FIRST THINGS FIRST

FIRST THINGS FIRST

A CONNOISSEUR'S COMPANION TO
BREAKFAST

RALPH POMEROY

PADDINGTON PRESS LTD
NEW YORK & LONDON

**Library of Congress Cataloging in
Publication Data**

Pomeroy, Ralph, 1926–
    First things first.

    Includes index.
    1. Breakfasts.   I. Title.
TX733.P65   394.1′2   76-53317
ISBN 0-448-22835-1

Printed in England by
BAS Printers Limited, Wallop, Hampshire
Bound by Garden City Press Ltd.,
London & Letchworth
Designed by Colin Lewis
Original illustrations by John Allen
For literary acknowledgments see page 154

IN THE UNITED STATES
PADDINGTON PRESS LTD.
Distributed by
GROSSET & DUNLAP

IN THE UNITED KINGDOM
PADDINGTON PRESS LTD.

IN CANADA
Distributed by
RANDOM HOUSE OF CANADA LTD.

IN AUSTRALIA
Distributed by
ANGUS & ROBERTSON PTY. LTD.

Contents

Personally

Breakfast is not everyone's cup of tea (or coffee). It is *some* people's cup of tea—and fruit juice and fried egg and bacon and toast and jam as well. Adam and Eve, those primary persons, didn't seem to worry about food at any time of day, cared for as they were by Miracle Management. But we more ordinary mortals usually want to eat something not too long after we wake up.

In the case of Darius and Xerxes, kings of Persia, the new day began with foods very dear to the hearts of today's health-food faddists—yogurts and melons, marmalades of thick honey, fruits of all kinds, nuts, spices and herbs. Kublai Kahn had fermented mare's milk for breakfast and perhaps meat cooked under his saddle—raw meat wedged under the saddle was "cooked" by friction as the rider galloped across the steppes. Louis XIV breakfasted lightly, at eight—bread and wine diluted with water. No doubt to save himself for the enormous meals he ate the remainder of the day.

My own memories of breakfast go back to early childhood in Illinois—I couldn't eat it. Nervous and ill, I spent one year in bed. Eggs made me throw up. My mother, either with wonderful instinct or the advice of a good doctor, got nourishment into me by beating raw eggs into fresh orange juice (when oranges were available) or into milk flavored with chocolate. I can still recall the unpleasant metallic taste of the albumen. The rest is confused.

Except I realize how lucky I was in terms of the freshness of the things I ate. Our house was in the middle of an orchard—apples in front, cherries in back. To this day I have never tasted apples as crisp, sweet, juicy and aromatic as those off the trees along our driveway. We called them "Snow Apples" and traded them to our farmer neighbors (we were suburb folk on the run from Depression losses) for eggs and potatoes and corn. Milk and butter and other dairy products we got from the milkman. But of course in that environment they were farm-fresh too.

Two other foods loom large in my mind from that time: my mother's exceptional French toast and her doughnuts. The secret of her French toast was that she toasted the bread (white) before dipping it into the mixture of egg and milk. This kept the bread from being soggy. We ate it with masses of butter and a generous dusting of powdered sugar or Log Cabin syrup. The doughnuts were—and still are, alas—the best I ever had: light yet dense. We children especially loved to eat the "holes" as soon as we could handle them, draining off the hot fat and sprinkling them with powdered sugar.

Then there is a big gap. A period in the army, stationed in Texas, was notable for horrendous powdered eggs, delicious "shit-on-a-shingle" (chipped beef, creamed, on toast), and a variety of freshly baked breads (each company had its own baker!). But it was my first trip to Britain that exposed me to the finest breakfasts I've ever eaten.

Along with two friends—all three of us still trying to get the military life out of our minds in 1947, I traveled through England and Scotland chiefly by bicycle for a summer and fall. Even without things like oranges (those were being sold one at a time to women in queues who gave them like crown jewels to children who had never seen one before), there were the "Bed and Breakfasts" with cheerful landladies—my first experience of fried bread and grilled tomatoes, my first exposure to awful cold dry toast. During this trip I experienced my first kipper and liked the taste so much I didn't mind dealing with all the bones. It was in Scotland that I came upon superb home-made jams and marmalades, eggs collected from hens only a short time before cooking. I remember even now the wonderful freshly baked bread and the fruit-heavy jam of a lady on the island of Skye; the farm breakfast, outside a town where we had finally found a place to sleep, which included a steamy curiosity I've always thought of as haggis but suspect was a superior example of blood sausage.

So, when I returned to America, I was changed forever. I became conscious of my father's ritual (my mother had died) of never-varying breakfast: one-half grapefruit, two slices of crisp bacon, two slices of wholewheat or raisin toast, one or two eggs soft-boiled or poached served in an egg cup or placed on toast. I was fascinated by the telling difference between the British preference for things fried in fat

(necessitated by the cold climate?) and my father's fastidious avoidance of it. My father continued to eat that breakfast the rest of his life. He never suffered any major illnesses until those of old age ended his life at eighty-four.

My breakfast was meager and one of mood—coffee with milk and "sweet rolls" (it was only when I moved to New York that I learned to call them "Danish") or scrambled eggs with bacon or sausages, toast. Once in a while a bowl of Rice Krispies with cream and sugar and perhaps a banana sliced over the top. On "good days" the beloved French toast. This usually turned out to be a Sunday when I wasn't hung over and was ritually accompanied by the Sunday paper. *That* was in New York, which I moved to in 1950. But between there and the Chicago suburb of Hubbard Woods, I made my first journey to France and Italy and nothing was to be the same ever again.

In neither country did people appear to eat breakfast. In Paris there was the discovery of glorious *croissants* and *brioches* and the flutes of just-baked bread called *baguettes*. These were adorned by marvelous butter and tart jams or honey and washed down with huge cups of foaming "half-and-half"—half pungent, slightly bitter coffee (my first taste of chicory), half

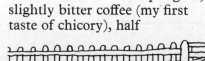

hot milk, and both always poured in tandem. That became my morning meal for quite a spell. Once though, with friends, I do remember eating plump golden peaches popping with juice sitting out under trees overlooking a summer sea near a place called Pont du Raz. Another time in Paris, perhaps homesick a bit, I ordered baked eggs in a café kitty-corner to the lovely ancient church of St.-Germain-des-Prés. They came in the two-handled dish they'd been cooked in, nestling on a slice of ham and shrouded in their buttery whites.

It was definitely homesickness that led myself and my best friend Fred Kuh—who was living in Paris too—to throw an "American Breakfast" for our American and French friends. This we held in a studio apartment on the ground floor of a very romantic enclave of studios on the Rue Boissonade. As crazy as it sounds we had been sent various items from America by Fred's mother. Our menu included bananas with cream and sugar, scrambled eggs and bacon, toast with butter and jam. It was a disaster as far as our French friends were concerned. They couldn't *believe* the bananas and cream and were revolted by the idea of eating eggs and bacon at the same time as toast and jam. It was my first serious lesson about the rigidity of French eating habits.*

I remember nothing special about Italian breakfast except for the freshness of the bread and the difference in the coffee. Basically it came two ways—*espresso*, exactly named: made very fast, the beans ground for each small cup, and drunk very fast; and *cappucino*: also individually ground but with the addition of steam-boiled milk making a lovely froth on which cinnamon or chocolate were dusted.

Outside of the home, coffee in the States was always a problem to me after this exposure to the French and Italian versions. Coffee in England had been appalling, but the tea was often memorable. Always, in my experience, served with milk which was traditionally poured into the cup first.

These liquids and the breads and, in the case of Britain, other foods that went with them, were my foreign and formative breakfast. When I first went to New York to live I worked in the mail room (required of all executives-to-be) of a big firm and lived in a cold-water flat in the East Forties. When I got depressed and was seized by a longing for Europe I would dress in my best suit and go to the Plaza Hotel on Sunday morning. There I would luxuriate in one of the deep, leather-upholstered banquettes in the Oak Room and eat grilled trout or poached sole with half a bottle of white wine, *café au lait* and the *Sunday Times*. The rest of the week it was peanut butter and jelly.

* Recently quite a revolution in these habits seems to be taking place. The *Guardian* (March 18, 1976) reported tea gaining popularity all over France, and the French fashion magazine *Elle* suggested in its April 1976 issue a more nutritious breakfast consisting of tea or coffee without milk (!), fruit or fruit juice, cheese, yogurt, toast, and *even* ham and eggs: "*Un tel petit déjeuner n'est pas contraire à la ligne.*"

The Eight O'Clock Peril

The poet Ogden Nash has a special talent for poking fun at practically every known form of human activity and breakfast is no exception. Here is his poem on the subject:

Breakfast is an institution that I don't know who commenced it,
But I am not for it, I am against it.
It is a thoroughly inedible repast.
And the dictionary says it is derived from the words break, meaning to break, and fast, meaning fast, so to breakfast means to break your fast.
Well that just shows how far you can trust a dictionary.
Because I never saw a definition that was more utterly fictionary.
The veriest child could see it doesn't check,
Because if the first syllable of breakfast means to break, why is it pronounced brek?
Shame on you, you old lexicographers, I shall call you laxicographers because you have grown very lax,
Because it is perfectly obvious that the first syllable in breakfast is derived from the far-famed Yale football cheer, which is Brekekekex co-ax co-ax,
And did you even get the second syllable right? Why a thousand times No,
Because the fast in breakfast doesn't mean fast, abstinence from food, it means fast, not slow.
So with that in mind we can peek behind the scenes
And then we can see what break-fast means,
It means that if you wake up in the morning feeling unappetizied and sickly,
Why you are confronted by a meal and the entire Yale football team coaxes you with an axe to eat it quickly.
On this topic I could write a chapter,
But I will content myself with saying that the French word for breakfast, which is *déjeuner*, is considerably apter,
Because it is perfectly truthful,
Because it is made up of the words *de*, meaning to un something, and *jeuner*, which must be derived from the word *jeune*, meaning young, so *jeuner* must mean to grow youthful,
So I think that is the reason that the French are always bright and gay,
Because they never eat breakfast because they are warned off it by their word for it, which means something that if you eat it you will grow unyouthful right away.

Starting

We don't know anything about the beginning of breakfast as such. We do know a little about what was eaten. History more or less starts with the written records of Sumer. Sumer tablets in Babylon refer to foods known to us now. Two or three thousand years before Christ complaints were lodged by the religious against civic dignitaries. They were accused of ploughing up the onion and cucumber patches claimed by the Temple. Garlic and chickpeas are mentioned, lentils, turnips, lettuce, leeks, mustard, cress and various beans. Thyme, pears and figs are listed as medicinal and to be mixed with beer or oil. Sumer literature mentions lambs and goats, cows and milk, fat, sheep, birds' eggs, fish, honey and wine. Grain is described as "in furrows." Pigs are known to have roamed the streets. Deer and wild boar were hunted. Birds were snared. Some fifty kinds of fish are recorded. Irrigation was well developed. Barley was the main crop. Sesame was cultivated for its oil. The world being smaller than we think when it comes to food and time, the agricultural workers of Sumer, circa 3000 B.C., ate barley cakes, onions and beer. Compare this with the bread, cheese and beer eaten by their nineteenth-century counterparts in England.

It was the Egyptians with their wheat crops who discovered raised bread. Before that bread was fashioned from flour mixed with water, some flavorings, and made into a flat cake. Later variations are the Mexican *tortilla* (corn or maize), the Indian *chapatis* (wheat), the Scots oatcake (oats). Way back then the Egyptians, like some California gold prospector treasuring his sourdough starter, kept back some of each day's dough to use as the raising agent for the next day's bread. Wheat was the reason for their success. Rye had not yet been cultivated and oats, barley and millet are not very satisfactory for making raised bread. Hard as it may be to believe, our commonplaces of bread—poppy seeds, sesame, etc.—were known and used along with things like honey, butter, eggs and milk which were mixed with the dough. Around 1500 B.C. bread ovens appeared and a great variety of breads were produced. There were round loaves and oval loaves, conical loaves and plaited ones. Workers were paid with bread and beer—so many loaves and jugs a day. Beer was *the* drink in ancient Egypt and was made from baked barley dough soaked in date-sweetened water and allowed to ferment. It is easy to imagine an Egyptian breakfast.

Meanwhile the Indians were busy growing wheat and barley of their own. The Chinese grew wheat and millet. Around 1000 B.C. barbarian nomads began to settle around the Aegean and Mediterranean seas, and what was to become Greece and Rome began. The Greeks preferred cattle to grain so they grew a little barley and imported their wheat. Their basic diet consisted of olives, fish, barley meal and wine, with meat on special occasions. The poet

Hesiod mentions goat's milk, kid and the "flesh of an uncalved heifer." Homer, in the *Iliad* describes a meal in which goat's milk cheese is grated into a cup of wine and sprinkled with white barley. A side dish consisting of an onion, honey and barley meal accompanies it. In another passage Achilles joins his companions in a meal of sheep, goat and a "great hog rich in lard" roasted on an open fire, sprinkled with "holy salt" and eaten with bread.

Things changed by the fifth century B.C. and a number of treatises appeared having to do with food. By the fourth century B.C. a man named Archestratus who styled himself as the inventor of "made" dishes, roamed the known world looking for information about food and drink in order to write about them. A great variety of fruits and vegetables were available. There were sauces and spices and dishes like stew. Pepper and rice were being imported from India. Olive oil and wine were being exported.

In the case of the Romans, although they—or at least the rich among them—ate an enormous variety of foods, they knew nothing of coffee, tea or chocolate, did not drink cow's milk or use cream or butter in their cooking (although the latter was imported from France for medicinal purposes). Strangely, they were aware of rice and sugar but did not use either. Oats were considered only as suitable food for horses.

Bread was a likely part of the standard Roman

fare. And, like the Egyptians, the Romans were inventive and produced a great variety of breads. Pliny speaks of bread named after the dishes eaten with it—"oyster-bread," "cake-bread"—or from its method of baking—"oven-bread," or "tin-loaf bread," or "baking-pan bread." Eggs and milk were sometimes kneaded into the dough. And, he tells us, "even butter has been used by races enjoying peace, when attention can be devoted to variety in pastry making." Professional bakers appeared on the scene around 171–168 B.C. Before that bread was made at home by women.

Around 500 A.D. the great Venetian trade was flourishing and salt was king. Which led quite

ABOVE: *An illustration from Alexis Soyer's* Pantropheon *(1853), showing the ancient Egyptians tending their wheat.*

naturally to such things as salted meat and fish and to the spices so crucial to the preparation of stored foods. The whole of Europe was involved. The Arabs, spreading the word of the Prophet, had taken over Egypt, Persia, North Africa, most of Spain and the Languedoc area. Their basic diet consisted of barley, mutton, dates and sheep's milk. Pork was forbidden along with all intoxicating liquors. During the horrors of the ninth and tenth centuries thousands of people died from poisoned rye made into bread and cannibalism was widespread in both France and Germany. The Swedes were eating biscuits made mostly from reindeer blood mixed with flour. The French were surviving on acorn bread.

In the beginning of the present era in India, two meals a day were advised as the best schemes. Each should consist of thirty-two mouthfuls. The stomach was to be considered as being divided into four parts—two to be filled with food, one with liquid, and one left empty to allow for wind. A typical meal might be made up of some ginger and salt to start, boiled rice and bean soup, hot butter sauce, some cakes with *ghee* (clarified buffalo butter), fruit and sugar cane. The very rich might eat pomegranates, grapes, oranges, mangoes, dates, spiced meat rolled in meat paste and rice, sweet cakes, spiced boiled rice, broth. This might be followed by curds and a milk liquor containing honey and sugar and a touch of saffron for color.

Unlike the Indians, the Chinese did not boil their rice. Quite early on—around the eighth century B.C.—they began steaming it. People became gourmets of rice, discussing the merits of pink rice, yellow rice and winter rice in much the same way they talked of Jewel tea, White Clouds tea or a tea known as Forest of Fragrance. They ate numerous fruits including peaches, pears, plums, cherries, chestnuts, melons, tangerines and mulberries. No doubt these foods figured in the morning meal. On the other hand, as dairy farming has never been a feature of Chinese life, milk, cream and butter were rarely used.

As for North America, the settlers of Virginia found the Indians making cakes from boiled and ground maize pounded into a paste. The Indian name for these "broad cakes" was *apone*, which became "corn pone" in the mouths of the newcomers. This was the nearest thing to American bread the first settlers knew. The New Englanders learned how to make hominy (a kind of porridge or pudding made from coarse corn meal) and succotash (a kind of purée which includes beans and boiled corn). Baked beans began with the Indians too. They seasoned their food with molasses or maple syrup instead of salt, which was rare. This could explain the sweetness of a number of American dishes. Corn was the staple food for the pioneers. They would have had to wait a year for wheat to grow and be harvested which would have slowed

down their journey hopelessly. So they grew corn. It was ready in about six weeks and didn't require ploughing or hoeing. A fascinating example of early "convenience food" was dried corn. Another was bean porridge, which housewives hung out to freeze in winter. All they had to do was to break off a piece, melt it down and serve. And there were "johnny-cakes"—from the Indian "shawnee" or "journey" cake. Cornmeal pancakes also kept for fairly long periods. There was even something called "pocket soup" which was an aspic of concentrated veal stock or cheap meat combined with pig's trotters. You simply dissolved a piece of it in hot water like a bouillon cube.

Obviously, many of these foods featured in people's first meal of the day.

Le Déjeuner, *Boucher's charming painting of a family breakfast in eighteenth-century France.*

In England Once

> There were three ravens sat on a tree,
> They were as black as they can be.
>
> The one of them said to his make,
> "Where shall we our breakfast take?"
>
> *Traditional*

In medieval England two meals were considered sufficient for a day which began at five in the morning and ended at nine at night. The first meal, or "dinner," was eaten at nine A.M., the second around five P.M. The salt cellar was crucial at table, its placement dividing those of "honourable estate" from the commoners and small fry. Hospitality flourished and was lavish not to say excessive, the tables of the castles being open to strangers as freely as to their vassals and followers. Food was not only tasty but attractive—birds "in their coffins" (forerunner of our modern pie), especially the spectacular peacock, were much favored. It is true, however, that masses of spices were used to cover up tainted fowl and game. Food was usually served as a kind of stew, with meat cut up into small pieces (there were no forks yet, remember) and spiced with extremely costly pepper and nutmeg, mace and clove. Often the meat was colored as well with sunflower seeds, parsley, mulberry juice and saffron. Vegetables were hardly used at all—it was considered socially degrading to eat them!

According to Frederick Hackwood in *Good Cheer*, the morning meal was very ceremonial with grace chanted and trumpeters announcing various dishes which might include "beef and mutton, fresh and salted, fowls and fish, pasties and loaves, wastel and simnel bread, numerous desserts . . . beeves, sheep, pigs, geese, fowls, venison and game . . . washed down with copious draughts of English ale and foreign wine. . . . For three hours or more the company sat entertained by jesters, tumblers, jugglers and buffoons and minstrels in the gallery."

In the fifteenth century gentlefolk breakfasted at seven on bread, beef, ale and wine. The journal of Elizabeth Woodville (who became Edward IV's queen) notes: "10 May 1451—Six o'clock (A.M.). Breakfasted. The buttock of beef rather too much boiled, and the ale a little the stalest. Memorandum: to tell the cook about the first fault, and to meet the second myself by tapping a fresh barrel directly."

The bread eaten at this time was made from a mixture of rye and wheat. Barley was used chiefly for making ale. "The Maner and Rytes of the Walshman" from the work called *Polycronycum* states:

> They ete brede colde and hote
> Of barley and of ote
> Brode cakes rounde and thynne
>
> Selde they ete brede of whete

A typical country scene in nineteenth-century England: a family gathered together for the first meal of the day— and one schoolboy trying to catch up on his homework.

They have gruell to potage
And leke is kind to companage
Also butter mylke and chese
Y shape endlong and cornerwese
Such messes they ete snell [quickly] . . .

L. F. Salzmann in *Medieval English Industries* writes of mealtimes in the building trade. In summer, for instance, work began at four A.M. and continued until seven P.M. At six A.M. there was a fifteen-minute break for refreshment, and at eight A.M. half an hour for breakfast. During the winter men worked from dawn until dusk, with half an hour for breakfast at nine A.M. In the good periods food was often thrown into the bargain.

The Tudor townsmen ate three meals a day. Breakfast, eaten around six or seven A.M., usually consisted of bread, salted or pickled herrings, cold meat, pottage, a kind of soup or stew, cheese and ale. Henry Best, a seventeenth-century writer, described a Yorkshire farm worker's pay which was partially in food: "Thatchers have in most places 6d. a day and theire meat in summer time . . . yett we never used to give them above 4d. . . . because their dyett is not as in other places . . . three meale a day, viz. theire breakfast att eight of the clock . . . fower services, viz. butter, milke, cheese, and either eggs, pycs, or bacon and sometimes porridge instead of milke. . . ."

The middle classes in the seventeenth century breakfasted between six and seven o'clock on cold meat, fish, cheese, dried or salted herrings, ale and beer. The famous diarist Samuel Pepys had friends over for a New Year's breakfast which consisted of "a barrel of oysters, a dish of meat's tongues, and a dish of anchovies, wine of all sorts and Northdowne Ale." Dr. Johnson in the eighteenth century was told by an Irish painter that £30 a year was sufficient to live on in London without being contemptible. He allowed "ten pounds for cloaths and linen . . . he might dine for 6d., breakfast on bread and milk for 1d., and do without supper . . . on clean shirt days he went abroad and paid visits. . . ."

In the early eighteenth century the poor, according to a workhouse account of the period for Bishopsgate, London, ate as follows: "They have Breakfasts, dinners and suppers every day in the week. For each meal 4 oz. of bread, $1\frac{1}{2}$ oz. cheese, 1 oz. butter, 1 pint of beer. Breakfast four days, bread and cheese or butter and beer. Monday a pint of pease pottage, with Bread and Beer. Tuesdays a Plumb Pudding Pye, 9 oz., and beer. Wednesdays a pint of frumity [hulled wheat boiled in milk and seasoned with cinnamon or sugar]. On Friday a pint of barley broth and bread. On Saturdays a plain flower suet Dumpling with beer. . . ." Sir Frederick Eden, writing in 1797, observed of this earlier period that workhouse food was actually better than that an industrious laborer could afford at home. Which was still true at the time he wrote. The weekly diet was:

Sunday, bread and cheese; Monday, broth; Tuesday, bread and cheese; Wednesday, same as Monday; Thursday, same as Tuesday; Friday, same as Monday; Saturday, bread and cheese. Eden found in 1794 at Heckingham, Norfolk, the diet was: Sunday, bread and cheese and butter or treacle; Monday, same as Sunday; Tuesday, milk and water gruel and bread; the rest of the week, the same as Sunday. Men were allowed a pint of beer at any meal except when they had broth or gruel. Nursing mothers were allowed the same.

In Robert Owens's autobiography he describes his life as a shop assistant in 1786 with Flint and Palmer, a haberdasher on the Borough side of London Bridge. He was fifteen. He received room and board in the house plus £25 a year: "The assistants were up and had breakfasted and were dressed to receive customers at 8 o'clock. . . . Dinner and tea were hastily taken—two or three, sometimes only one escaping at a time to take whatever he or she could the most easily swallow. . . . The only regular meals at this time were our breakfasts, except on Sundays, on which days a good dinner was always provided and much enjoyed." It is worth noting that the shop assistants were often up until one in the morning tidying up.

A man named Aiken writing in 1795 pictures a clothing manufacturer's morning in Manchester: He "used to be in his warehouse before six in the morning, accompanied by his children and apprentices. At seven they all came in to breakfast, made of oatmeal and water and a little salt, boiled thick. . . . At the side was a basin of milk. And the masters and apprentices, each with a wooden spoon in his hand, without loss of time dipped into the same dish, and thence into the milk pan: and as soon as it is finished, they all returned to work. . . ."

The Children's Diet in Christ Church Hospital, London, in 1704 consisted of bread and beer for breakfast every day. The Foundling Hospital in 1747 did somewhat better by its inmates. Breakfast for the week was—Sunday, broth; Monday, gruel; Tuesday, milk porridge; Wednesday, broth; Thursday, gruel; Friday, milk porridge; Sunday, gruel. The staff breakfasted on milk, milk porridge, rice milk or bread and cheese. Fifteen years later the children were at least getting bread and butter on Sundays and bread and milk on Wednesdays and Saturdays. In 1793 inmates at Carlisle workhouse got Hasty Pudding (a thick batter of flour stirred in boiling milk or water) with milk or beer for their breakfast.

The horrors of child labor during the Industrial Revolution were vividly described by the children themselves during an inquiry into their working conditions. A ten-year-old boy working a twelve-hour day was allowed a half hour for breakfast, an hour at noon and another half hour "drinking time." But, and this was true for all the children, the machines often had to be cleaned during these same

One of the many "coffee taverns" established in England during the 1870s. The idea was to supply working men with an alternative to the public house and— instead of spirits—coffee, tea or cocoa at the start of the day.

periods. In at least one case, the overseer put the clock forward while the children were trying to eat and they had to stop and run back to work. There was a great deal of dust in the mill in question and it was impossible to "take food out of your basket or handkerchief but what it is covered with dust directly . . . they will not allow us the time, and we have to bolt our food as we can. . . . If they were allowed a little time to get their breakfast and 'drinking' in, they could then go out of doors and get the meat clean and comfortable, and the dust would not get into it."

A girl named Elizabeth Bentley reported that she started work at six and that the only time allowed for "drinking" or breakfast or *any* meal in fact was a forty-minute period at mid-day. One parent tells of his children going to the mills at three A.M. and returning after ten P.M. During these nineteen hours a quarter of an hour was allowed for breakfast, a half hour for dinner and another quarter hour for drinking. But there was always the business of cleaning the machines: "They generally had to do what they call 'dry down': sometimes this took the whole of the time at breakfast or drinking, and they were to get their dinner or breakfast as they could." When asked about the problem of waking his children to go to work, the man explained that he and his wife dressed the children still asleep on their feet and that his wife often "stopped up all night, for fear we could not get them ready for the time." They both got up at two A.M. to get the children off so that the most sleep the children could possibly get was about four hours. The father goes on to say: "We have cried often when we have given them the little victualling we had to give them. We had to shake them and they have fallen to sleep with the victuals in their mouths many a time."

Nor were adults spared. In 1825 an anonymous reporter published *A Sketch of the Hours of Labour, Mealtimes, etc, etc., in Manchester and its Neighbourhood*, which revealed that "the hours of labour at present seem, on the average, about fourteen. The greater number of mills allow half an hour for breakfast. . . . There are others, however, which allow no time for breakfast." The reporter visited a large number of other places—among them Stockport, Leeds and Hatfield—and found the hours from fourteen to fifteen and the breakfast half hour allowed only at very few mills.

The mines were equally appalling. Children as young as four were employed to sit in the dark from dawn till dusk opening and shutting trapdoors. Older ones hauled trucks. Men worked naked, and women and girls naked to the waist. As a general rule miners were allowed no time at all for meals. An official report dated 1842 notes: "In the majority of the coal districts of England, Scotland and Wales, no regular time whatever is even nominally allowed for meals, but the people have to take what little food they eat during their long hours of labour when they best can snatch a moment to swallow it."

There ensued a tremendous struggle against people who thought themselves respectable and of the highest moral principles before an increasingly outraged public brought about legislation to limit the hours of women and children and finally to abolish child labor altogether. There were of course a few enlightened and humane employers. George Unwin in *Samuel Oldknow and the Arkwrights* relates that at Mellon Mill, run by Samuel Oldknow, a contemporary named Robert Blincoe observed that the apprentices seemed cheerful and looked healthy and that they ate "milk porridge and wheaten bread for breakfast and that their meals were good and sufficient." Many years later a descendant of one of these apprentices told of her mother's life in the "prentice" house. According to her they exercised every day in the meadows in front of the house, and "had porridge and bacon for breakfast, meat every day for dinner, pudding or pies on alternate days, and when pigs were killed were regaled with meat pies which were full of meat and had a short crust. All the fruit in the orchard was eaten by the children. . . ."

Engels, Karl Marx's collaborator, wrote of the working-class life during the 1840s—and other people's evidence shows that he did not exaggerate for political reasons: "Descending gradually, we find the animal food reduced to a small bit of bacon cut up with potatoes; lower still, even this

19

disappears, and there remain only bread, cheese, porridge and potatoes, until on the lowest round of the ladder, among the Irish, potatoes form the sole food." Remember breakfast had to come out of this day's rations. Engels tells us of the London poor collecting potato parings, rotten vegetables and vegetable refuse in order to augment their diet.

In the last century, the average English public school breakfast consisted of bread and butter, beer or tea. Supper was the same. The students had to supplement their diet with boxes from home or at "tuck shops" in order to get enough nourishment. Such was the situation of the so-called privileged class.

At the same time there *were* companies under enlightened management with good kitchens and dining rooms where food could be got at cost. One of these was Cadbury's, the cocoa and chocolate manufacturers, as reported in 1899 by an American named Nicholas Paine Gilman. In his study, *A Dividend to Labour*, Cadbury's was said to absorb "one-third of all the cocoa imported in England" at that time. September to December the hours in the factory were 6 A.M. to 5:30 P.M. (1 P.M. on Wednesday and 12:30 P.M. on Saturday. "The girl arriving so early receives a cup of tea and a biscuit. She is allowed half an hour for breakfast, fifteen minutes for lunch, and one hour for dinner. For the other months of the year the hours are from 8:45 A.M. to 5:30 P.M.—1:30 P.M. on Saturday." At

Fry's, the oldest cocoa firm in the world, founded in 1728, conditions were equally good. Perhaps the fact that both firms were owned by Quakers had something to do with it. Much the same enlightened policy was pursued in certain companies both in the United States and on the Continent during this period.

According to another study of industrial catering—*Model Factories and Villages* by Budgett Meakin (1905)—Messrs. Guinness and Son "provide a large dining room, at which a staff of cooks and attendants are maintained at their expense, the cost price of the food alone being charged. Workmen on special tasks receive free meals. Draymen starting early get substantial breakfasts free, and those starting at 6 A.M., including the women cleaners, are supplied with roll and tea or coffee free."

In 1913 the Chief Inspector of Factories reported that one firm not far from Dundee, which employed five hundred to six hundred men, provided a breakfast "of porridge and milk $1\frac{1}{2}$d, tea $\frac{1}{2}$d per large cup, roll and margarine $\frac{1}{2}$d, eggs at current prices." By 1916—and with a war on—the *practical* side of feeding workers properly was being openly acknowledged. The Canteen Committee of the Central Control Board put out a booklet entitled "Feeding the Munition Worker," which stated: "There is now an overwhelming body of evidence and experience which prove that productive output in regard to quality, amount and speed is largely dependent upon the physical efficiency and health of the worker. In its turn much physical fitness is dependent upon nutrition, the purpose of which is to secure the proper development, growth and energy of the human body. . . . What is the necessary diet for the worker? . . . A sufficient quantity of nutritive material in proper proportions. Suitably mixed. Easily digestable. Appetizing and attractive. Obtainable at low cost." Thus do officialdom and special interest arrive at the humanely obvious.

The lesson was well learned. In World War I only specific factories working in armaments were required by law to provide canteens. By World War II every factory over a certain size was required to have one. Nowadays canteens are pretty much a commonplace in offices and factories all over the world. Workers are provided with attractive, clean eating areas with decent food at nominal cost, and if the hours worked involve breakfast, then this is made available with a wide range of dishes to choose from—usually cafeteria style with a self-help set up. And the mid-morning "coffee or tea break" is notorious by now—so much so, that lots of firms prefer to bring the coffee or tea *to* the worker in order to keep him or her at their task instead of allowing them to go to a canteen or coffee bar. Not everyone is happy with this arrangement.

A coffee bar at Hyde Park Corner in London, where the end of the night meets the start of the day. A pencil drawing by Edward Burra, done in the 1930s.

Eggs

The egg is one of the most perfect and beautiful structures in nature. Its fragility is distributed throughout its form in such a way as to achieve maximum strength. Its shape makes the most of space. The great Rumanian sculptor Brancusi used its form as a metaphor for the new born. It hangs mysteriously above the Madonna in one of Pierro della Francesca's paintings. It is a kind of world with sun and cloud within. It is decorated and exchanged at Easter. Fabergé apotheosized it in jewels and precious metals.

In ancient days philosophers held eggs in special respect for they saw in them an emblem of the world and the four elements—the shell, earth; the white, water; the yolk, fire; the air, under the shell. Orpheus, Pythagorus and many others advocated abstaining from eating eggs in order to encourage the production of chickens. In India and Syria hens were worshiped though their eggs were eaten. The Greeks and Romans were superstitious about them

and used them in their religious rites. Nero's consort Livia consulted a sorceress about her forthcoming child and was told to warm a new-laid egg in her bosom and if a male chicken was hatched she would have a son. Livia followed her instructions and a cock chick emerged. Shortly afterwards she gave birth to Tiberius. A man dreamed he had eaten an egg and was told by a soothsayer that the white symbolized silver and the yolk gold and he would come into both soon. He did. Egyptian shepherds cooked eggs without fire—they put them in a sling and swung it so fast that the friction of the air heated the eggs to the exact degree they wanted. In Rome and Greece new-laid eggs were served at the beginning of meals and it was held that to maintain one's health "it was necessary to remain at table from the egg to the apple." The Romans fancied other than hens' eggs. They sought those of the partridge and pheasant and the gorgeous peacock. And, although they were partial to soft-boiled eggs, they cooked them in a variety of ways. At one time or another the English ate eggs laid by ducks, geese, plovers, guinea fowl, seagulls and wild birds like the heron, cormorant, raven and Peregrine falcon.

One should be careful with eggs. Above all they should be as fresh as possible. Ideally they should be produced by range-free hens. You can tell if an egg is fresh if it sinks when put into water. Contrary to some people's beliefs, the color of the shell or yolk has nothing to do with the quality. If kept in the refrigerator they should be stored away from strong-smelling foods as they absorb the smell of other foods easily.

Eggs contain high-quality protein—about seven grams—and about 88 calories. They also contain ten amino acids and calcium and iron. The yolks are one of the few food sources of Vitamin D. They offer a problem in that they also contain nearly the daily limit (300 grams) of cholesteral, but to counteract this it is claimed that with a diet high in vitamins B and C and lecithin one egg a day is all right.

In our own time there are a great number of ways to prepare eggs and for many of us the cries of short-order cooks resonate in memory: "Sunny side up!"—meaning not turned over, the opposite of "Once over lightly!" Or "Adam and Eve on a raft!"—two fried eggs on toast. There are fried eggs, poached eggs, scrambled eggs, coddled eggs, baked eggs, boiled eggs, omelettes and soufflés. Many cooks believe eggs are best cooked in glass or enamel pans and that a wooden spoon is the best utensil for stirring them. They also feel that eggs should be at room temperature when you go to cook them so it's best to take them out of the refrigerator at least an hour beforehand. Ideally, they should be cooked *slowly* over moderate heat and you should try to avoid overcooking.

Among the hundreds of ways to prepare eggs, a few of the basic ones are: *hard-boiled* (5–6 min.); *soft-boiled* (3–4 min.), with the larger part up, they're easier to open in an egg cup. *Poached eggs* are best with the egg broken into a saucer and slid into gently boiling water and cooked for about $2\frac{1}{2}$ minutes (or you can use an egg poacher). Eggs can also be poached in milk or broth. *Fried eggs* are best cooked in a heavy skillet in bacon fat or butter over moderate heat. Baste as they cook. To turn, use a slotted pancake turner. Give them another minute or so depending on how you like them. Drain off fat. *Scrambled*: low heat and lots of butter should keep them from getting rubbery. Cooking them in a double boiler helps too. Add about a tablespoon of water or cream for each egg. Beat only slightly.

Omelettes: Marvelous to eat but, to most of us, intimidating to cook. They require great care and attention to detail and should be allowed their own skillet. The true omelette cooker never uses his pan for anything else and he never washes it. The skillet is best when small (ideally, omelettes should be cooked one at a time)—about 6 to 8 inches across—and should be cleaned with salt and paper toweling. This may seem fanatical but it really works.

For an ordinary omelette, beat eggs with water or cream lightly. Pour into hot but not brown butter. When almost cooked but still creamy, roll over with a spatula and fold as you slide eggs onto a warm plate. One of the delightful things about omelettes is that you can add all sorts of things to them—mushrooms, cheese, chicken, peppers, lox, spinach, onions, tomatoes. Extras should be cooked be-

A six-egg boiling apparatus illustrated in the Magasin Pittoresque *(France, 1868).*

forehand if necessary and added just before folding. Season to taste.

A "fluffy" omlettte differs in that the eggs are separated. Beat yolks with milk and salt. Beat whites until stiff and then fold into the yolks. Cook slowly over low heat until omelette puffs up. Place in 400° F. oven until brown and cooked through (8–10 min.).

The dazzling French omelette is made in a skillet with rounded sides and requires considerable skill. It has to do with shaking the pan gently with one hand while the other whirls a fork. Pour well-beaten eggs into sizzling butter, begin double motion and continue for about $\frac{1}{2}$ minute. Allow to settle and set for a few seconds. Roll omelette over itself onto a warm plate. It should finish cooking with its own heat. Practice. Consult your cook book. Discuss with friends. Pray.

Here are some classic recipes:

James Beard's Eggs Florentine *(4 servings)*
Cook one package of frozen chopped spinach. Drain thoroughly, season to taste with salt and freshly ground pepper and blend in two tablespoons of butter. Spread the spinach in a shallow baking dish and top with eight poached eggs. Cover with Sauce Mornay (made by adding two or three tablespoons of grated Switzerland Swiss cheese or grated Parmesan or a mixture of both along with three tablespoons of heavy cream to a basic white sauce).

Then sprinkle with grated Parmesan and run under the broiler to brown.

Robert Carrier sprinkles his eggs with grated nutmeg and lemon juice before covering with the sauce.

Elizabeth David's Basque Pipérade
In a heavy frying or sauté pan melt some pork fat. (Olive oil is sometimes used for this dish, but pork, or even bacon fat, suits it better.) Put in one pound of sliced onions, and let them cook slowly until they turn golden but not brown. Then put in three fairly large sweet red peppers (or about six small green ones) cut into strips; let this cook until it is soft, then add one pound chopped tomatoes, and season with salt, ground black pepper and a little marjoram. Cook with the cover on the pan.

When the whole mixture has become almost the consistency of a purée, pour in six beaten eggs and stir gently, exactly as for ordinary scrambled eggs. Take care not to let them get overcooked.

Brochettes of calf's liver are sometimes served with Pipérade—and a very good combination it is.

Patricia Holden White's Basic Cheese Soufflé *(6 servings)*
Whisk together $\frac{1}{4}$ cup butter and $\frac{1}{4}$ cup flour over medium heat until smooth and add two cups milk, $\frac{1}{2}$ teaspoon salt, $\frac{1}{4}$ teaspoon white pepper, and a pinch of nutmeg. Continue whisking until thickened and

smooth. Stir in ¾ cup of grated Swiss cheese and ¾ cup grated Parmesan cheese and continue stirring until cheese is melted and the mixture smooth. Remove from heat and whisk in five egg yolks. Cool. Beat six egg whites until stiff and fold quickly into cheese mixture. Pour into buttered soufflé dish and bake at 375° F. for about 25 minutes, until well puffed and browned (*never* open oven to check!).

With garlic croutons: Sauté one clove of garlic in two tablespoons of olive oil. Add two slices of day-old bread, crusted and finely cubed, and sauté until browned. Drain and add to soufflé when folding in egg whites.

With bacon: Fry two slices of bacon until crisp. Drain well and crumble, adding to soufflé when folding in egg whites.

With chives: Add one tablespoon fresh or freeze-dried chives when folding in egg whites.

Eggs Benedict

More a way of serving eggs than a recipe. Use one English muffin and two poached eggs per person. Split and toast the muffins, top each with a slice of sautéed or boiled ham. Place egg on top of ham and cover with Hollandaise sauce.

"Temperance Enjoying a Frugal Meal": detail from a cartoon by Gillray dated 1792 in which George III is ironically taken to task for his meager meals.

Some People...

Two reporters—Wendy Law and Yone Seagrave—writing in March 1976 for that worthy gadfly among American newspapers, the *Washington Post*, reported on the early morning eating habits of a number of Washington notables. Gerald Ford ate around 6:30 A.M. (!) after exercising—fruit, toast or English muffin, and tea. Ronald Reagan, typically uptight, thinks people should sleep through the whole thing, although he's been known to drink orange juice (the California vote?). Henry Kissinger would meet over breakfast four out of five mornings. He began around eight and liked eggs, bacon, English muffin, juice, coffee. Ron Nessen, then Ford's press secretary, likes a good breakfast: large grapefruit juice, English muffin without butter, raisin bran with milk, coffee. Henry Jackson? Juice, all-bran, tea. Mo Udall always eats scrambled eggs, bacon, toast, orange juice, coffee, milk. Ralph Nader won't tell. A humorless spokesman states: "We do not feel that what he eats for breakfast is a pressing consumer interest." Averell Harriman eats only the white of his eggs, a habit shared by Strom Thurmond. Thurmond awakes to a glass of prune juice chased with hot water, goes for a jog of several miles, and returns to orange juice, grapefruit juice, milk, whole wheat toast—and the whites of two eggs, poached or beaten in his milk. Elliot Richardson has been known to eat the orthodox eggs, toast, black coffee, juice. Alice Roosevelt Longworth incredulously asked, "Do people still eat breakfast?"

William Proxmire, who seems more imaginative than most, has sardines, or tuna, or salmon—all low-fat protein and "tastes terrific."

Not really a surprise, the most inviting and elegant breakfast described is contributed by the great Katherine Anne Porter. She offers several menus: champagne and snails with crusty rolls and sweet butter; orange juice; coffee; veal with tarragon and shallots, sweet butter, and sour cream; button mushrooms and potato balls.

Thomas Jefferson would have understood. He was the kind of gourmet who went shopping daily with his French cook (and spent around $50!). On weekends he rose, dealt with his correspondence, took a walk, and then ate like a king: capitolade of fowl on toast, braised partridges with tartar sauce, tansy pudding (made from the bitter herb of that name), hot breads, cold meats, bacon, eggs, fried apples and batter cakes.

One hears more and more about the "working breakfast" made internationally famous by Henry Kissinger. It makes sense (unless of course you can't wake up) compared to blurred lunches or dozy dinners laced with booze and wine. French President Giscard d'Estaing recently celebrated the inaugural flight of Concorde by entertaining the crew at breakfast.

According to *Vogue* (November 5, 1968) men seem to have an "instinctive grasp of rules that govern health and well-being, and their direct sequel, good looks ... rules that even the most beauty-conscious women blithely ignore." It seems, says *Vogue*, that while women "rush out of the house with a cup of black coffee, or nothing at all, aboard," men "eat a jolly good breakfast." At least "notably attractive men do," men known "not only for their charm but their energy, their trim, unflabby figures, their general air of fitness and verve."

Of the answers they got to their investigation, some they found surprising. They decided to deal with three of the "most picturesque." Hardly a term I would have chosen to describe the late Duke of Windsor. Still, the Duchess graciously described His Royal Highness's eating habits at the start of his day. It seems he ate no lunch but enjoyed a hearty, late breakfast—mostly an English one modified towards French or American variations depending on where he was. There was always a glass of grapefruit juice to begin, "endless cups of tea during the meal, two vitamin pills after, if remembered."

Some of the menus the Duke liked: scrambled eggs with creamed haddock, scones; chicken hash with bacon, corn muffins; Kedgeree of turbot, salmon, haddock, or other fish, with chutney and curry sauce (the chutney had to be of mangoes and heated), a flat biscuit called *galette indienne*; eggs fried with cream, bacon and *croissants*; French white sausages (*Boudin blanc*) or, in America, German white sausages and mashed potatoes (suspiciously like the English common folk's "bangers and mash."

And always "some kind of bread or toast and orange marmalade."

Yul Brynner seems far more adventurous. Besides black coffee, he's been known to eat "a small-sized roasted chicken" or even "a leg of lamb of medium size." He might fancy scrambled eggs and a breast of chicken, with "a large scoop of caviar on the side." Or, in a hurry, he might choose "a piece of pineapple with cheese."

When asked, in an interview for *The Observer* (London) in the summer of 1975, how he spent his time, Jean-Paul Sartre answered rather gently, "My life has become very simple since I can't get about very much. I get up at half-past eight. I often sleep *chez* Simone de Beauvoir and I go home after breakfasting in a café on the way." Being a philosopher no doubt accounts for his not saying *what* he breakfasted *on*.

And athletes? Tennis champ Arthur Ashe, at a breakfast interview in London in July 1975, ordered porridge, two poached eggs, bacon, toast, jam, and coffee. Chris Evert, another tennis luminary, was reported by *Esquire* ("Breakfast of Champions," October 1974) as never missing breakfast—half a grapefruit with honey ("natural sugar is important" to her performance), two eggs, usually soft-boiled, one slice of whole wheat toast, occasionally bacon.

The *Esquire* piece proved nothing about athletes' eating habits except that they differ widely. Among the dozen sports figures discussed, nine drink orange

or grapefruit juice or have a half grapefruit and, more interestingly, only three of them drink coffee, none drink tea. Track star Cheryl Toussaint prefers a vanilla malted (sometimes with an egg). Billy Caspar doesn't eat breakfast when his starting time is before nine A.M. Otherwise he follows his grapefruit or juice with six ounces of ground beef or steak and half an avocado. Julius Erving only eats breakfast once or twice a week. He prefers to sleep late. He doesn't eat eggs, "avoids beans, milk, or too much soda before a game because they take their toll." When he does have breakfast he fancies canned fruit, cold cereal, toast, the occasional pancake. Boxer George Foreman gets up at seven when he's in training, does road work, naps, gets up at ten and has four or five eggs—poached, fried or scrambled—beef sausages (he doesn't think pork is good for him), a large glass of orange or grapefruit juice, several slices of whole wheat or rye bread. Mark Spitz almost always eats the same breakfast: orange juice, two eggs, white toast, sometimes sausages.

The jockey Bill Shoemaker can't ride on a full stomach so he doesn't eat again until dinner. When he's working it's juice, poached or scrambled eggs, one slice of cracked wheat bread, bacon or sausages, or four ounces of blood-rare steak, coffee with raw honey and cream, melon, "preferably papaya," multivitamins and vitamin E.

Reporter Merla Zellerback of the San Francisco *Chronical* did a story called "Breakfast, the Eccentric Meal" (November 10, 1975) in which she reported on the strange breakfasts enjoyed by a group of San Franciscans. Marcia Hill likes Heineken's beer. Robin Collins, a food writer, likes jamocha almond fudge or banana nut ice cream best of all, but if she's so moved she "whips up a dish called Picadillo—hamburger with chiles, walnuts and raisins, ice cream for dessert." Eric Johnson, an "auto man," favors chocolate cake followed by apple pie. With it he likes soup—"chicken noodle or minestrone." He finds one of the beauties of Tahoe is that people gamble all night and "you can order dinner for breakfast and no one even blinks." Cookbook author Micheline Beatty, with some justification, thinks gourmet eating shouldn't be limited to lunch or dinner. She chooses filet of sole Meunière or lamb kidneys with mushrooms, or quail on toast in season. "Instead of coffee cake—lemon crèpes with butter and powdered sugar." Adalene Ross, a fashion expert, starts with carrot juice and follows with a soft-boiled egg, wheat toast with Scotch marmalade, some watercress and tea with natural honey and can "go all day on it." Theater director Bill Ball eats three scrambled eggs and drinks a cold "Bieler soup" of green beans, zucchini, parsley and celery (a recipe of health authority Dr. Bieler).

In England, Frenchman Louis Frémaux who conducts the City of Birmingham Symphony

Orchestra, feels that the English are more sensible about rehearsals than his fellow countrymen. The French orchestras rehearse from nine to noon then take a two-hour break for lunch. In Birmingham they begin at "10:15 after the traffic jams have eased." At midday they have a short lunch break. This enables M. Frémaux to eat breakfast—"You see, I love the English breakfast, but I couldn't possibly eat that much if I was making an early start."

Robert Carrier, whose real name is MacMahon (Carrier is his middle name), recently recalled for an interviewer his boyhood breakfast of mashed strawberries in whipped cream—"A six-year-old's idea of cuisine."

Harry Secombe, the British actor, fondly recalls his childhood in Swansea in Wales where he ate laverbread, "made from seaweed and looking like cow pat." It was "always on sale in the market along with little bags of oatmeal. My mother used to cook it for Sunday breakfast with bacon and there is no taste as delicious in the world."

That maker of epic Westerns, John Ford, feels that "As you grow older, you develop a fondness for the food that you were brought up on, and my favorite is still baked beans—Maine baked beans. You eat them on a Saturday night, and then finish them on Sunday morning fried, before going to church."

Lilian Gish still loves ". . . apple sauce with cream over it . . . so luxurious to me at that time, to this day, I adore that dish in the mornings. Slice the apples and boil them in orange juice and serve without sugar and cover with cream."

Christopher Isherwood has a favorite breakfast cereal (as reported in *Nobs & Nosh* by Allen Warren, 1974): a mixture of a cup of filbert, another of cashew, a dish of dehydrated apples, chopped together and added to a cup of steel-cut oats, a two-pound bag of rolled oats, a cup each of powdered wheatgerm and raisins, and a small packet of grape-nuts. Mix together with milk.

Ian McEwan in a piece about Flaubert in the *Radio Times* wrote: "A quiet routine was established at Croisset, the beautiful house on the edge of the Seine where Flaubert lived with his mother and five-year-old niece. Physically it was a very comfortable formula, 'One must . . . live like a bourgeois and think like a God. The satisfactions of the mind and body have little in common.' The household had to remain silent till Flaubert woke, at 10 A.M. At the sound of his bedroom bell a servant scurried upstairs with a glass of water, a ready filled pipe, the morning post and the papers. Then Flaubert would thump on the wall or shout for his mother who would appear instantly from her room next door. She would sit by his bed till he was ready to get up. There followed a vast meal which combined breakfast with lunch."

...And Some Institutions

Most of us are familiar with institutional breakfasts—from school days to time spent in hospital—but not too many of us can say we know the kind of food one can expect to find being served in prison, at a military academy or in a super-submarine.

Breakfast at Sing Sing (officially Ossining Correctional Facility) or, in other words, prison, for the first week of February 1976 was as follows (the menus are signed by the food service manager, the steward, the physician and the superintendent):

Sun. Feb. 1	Grapenut Cereal, Milk and Sugar, Orange Juice, Bread and Butter, Coffee
Mon. Feb. 2	Rolled Oats Cereal, Milk and Sugar, Grapefruit Juice, Bread and Butter, Coffee
Tues. Feb. 3	Rice Krispies, Milk and Sugar, Orange Juice, Bread and Butter, Coffee
Wed. Feb. 4	(2) Hard Boiled Eggs, Hot Cereal, Grapefruit Juice, Bread and Butter, Breakfast Bun, Coffee
Thurs. Feb. 5	Farina Cereal, Milk and Sugar, $\frac{1}{2}$ Fresh Grapefruit, Bread and Butter, Coffee
Fri. Feb. 6	Bran Flakes, Milk and Sugar, Orange Juice, Raisin Bread and Butter, Coffee
Sat. Feb. 7	Grapefruit Cereal, Milk and Sugar, (1) Fresh Banana, Bread and Butter, Coffee

This would seem very low on protein and high on carbohydrates for starting off the day.

Cadets at the West Point Academy fare a good deal better. (*Their* menus are approved by the Cadet Mess Board and the Cadet Panel.) For the week ending February 1, 1976, the future officers of the U.S. Army were fed:

Mon. Jan. 26	Orange Juice, Assorted Dry Cereal, Frilled Ham Slice, Blueberry Waffles with Maple Syrup and Margarine, Assorted Jellies—Honey, Coffee—Milk
Tues. Jan. 27	Grape Juice, Assorted Dry Cereal, Hot Wheat Cakes with Maple Syrup and Margarine, Canadian Bacon, Assorted Jellies—Honey, Coffee—Milk
Wed. Jan. 28	Sliced Pears, Assorted Dry

Cereal, Spanish Omelette, Crumb Coffee Cake, Toast—Margarine—Apple Butter, Assorted Jellies—Honey, Box of Raisins, Coffee—Hot Chocolate—Milk

Thurs. Jan. 29 Sliced Peaches, Assorted Dry Cereal, Breakfast Steak, Scrambled Eggs, Home Fried Potatoes, Toast—Margarine, Assorted Jellies—Honey, Coffee—Milk

Fri. Jan. 30 Orange Juice, Assorted Dry Cereal, Strawberries and Vanilla Ice Cream, Country-Style Scrambled Eggs, Toast—Margarine, Bran Muffins, Assorted Jellies—Honey, Coffee—Milk

Sat. Jan. 31 Pineapple Juice, Assorted Dry Cereal, Cinnamon French Toast with Maple Syrup and Margarine, Smoked Sausage Links, Fruit Bowl, Assorted Jellies—Honey, Coffee—Milk

Sun. Feb. 1 BRUNCH: Orange Juice, Assorted Dry Cereal, Turkey à la King on Toast Points with Sliced Egg Garnish, French Fried Potatoes, Toast—

Margarine—Peanut Butter-filled Coffee Ring, Fruit Compote—Assorted Jellies—Honey, Coffee—Hot Chocolate—Milk

An impressive menu, full of variety. Only complaints: why no butter (unlike Sing Sing) or tea (like Sing Sing)?

The crew of a British Polaris submarine eats food prepared by "hotel-trained chefs" in nuclear-powered kitchens. Favorites are "Yellow Peril" (kippers) and "Train Smash" (mixed grill). It's more difficult to learn what Her Majesty's Life Guards eat. In answer to my query, a lieutenant-colonel of the Household Cavalry, the Horse Guards, wrote only that "officers are permitted to partake of breakfast wearing their uniform hat" but that the " 'privilege' is rarely exercised." Breakfast is run on a buffet basis and "all officers do not sit down to the meal at the same time." As to what they *eat*, I haven't a clue.

The Discreet Charm...

There are not many humble meals depicted in art. Breakfasts least of all. True, over the centuries, we have been shown a number of peasants breaking bread—especially in the nineteenth century—but the emphasis has been on feast days and weddings as in Bruegel and Veronese. Of course we have had great images of the Last Supper and other suppers as well—most notably that famous one at Emmaus. And we have had any number of picnics—most notably that *in*famous one by Manet. But no paintings of breakfast leap, as those do, to the mind. Not before the twentieth century that is. Not before Bonnard.

For the fact of the matter is that the great Frenchman, Pierre Bonnard, born in the sixties of the last century and having died in the forties of this one, produced a series of breakfast paintings spanning the whole of his career. Among several subjects particularly loved and painted by him again and again—women in bathtubs, gardens, baskets or bowls of flowers and fruit—the "altars" of the dining room were marvelously captured.

As James Thrall Soby remarked in *Bonnard and His Environment* (1964), he liked "uncomplicated domesticity." Food was an important part of that domesticity and he painted it repeatedly. "Not food as prepared by the great restaurants of France so much as food prepared at home by skilled housewife or maid," says Soby. However, unlike the Dutch Little Masters of the seventeenth century who enjoyed painting food as well, but food waiting to be cooked, Bonnard was more interested in the meal itself, along with its aftermath: many of his paintings show a table half-cleared, *after* the food has been eaten.

Lover of the domestic, the intimate, the private, the sensual, no wonder Bonnard was drawn so often to that most private of all domestic meals—breakfast. In most of his morning pictures there is only one person shown—a woman, most often Marthe de Méligny who became his wife. This figure sits musing over her cup (actually, in the French manner, there isn't all that much *food*), drawn up very close to the rather high table. Her hands, resting on the edge of the table, come to above her breast. There are small bowls about, pitchers, tins and baskets. There is a favorite, brown ceramic pot. Heaps of fruit set up rainbow harmonies. Sometimes a dog sits in her lap or waits for food nearby. Sometimes a cat strains a paw toward some morsel. This tolerance of animals *à table* adds to the authenticity of the scene—to its air of a thing being observed without any self-consciousness. We, the invading strangers, are invisible. Therefore no need for pretense. The animals reinforce this air of extreme privacy—no hiding away of socially bad habits. They also increase the mood of sensuality and freedom: fun is added to flowers and fruit; the forbidden tested.

In *The Breakfast Room*, in the collection of the

# of Pierre Bonnard

Museum of Modern Art in New York, the morning is presented to us like a play. The proscenium is a large, three-part window through which we see, first a balustrade, second a sky-oozing wealth of branches and foliage, and lastly, a path leading to a fence and several small figures. But it is a play *within* a play. The major drama is taking place *before* the window. Here the proscenium is the edge of the painting itself and the stage is chiefly a white and pale-blue tablecloth. At center stage there sits an empty cup which serves to place us as an audience. We (from Bonnard's viewpoint) are seated there apparently alone, although there is a glass (of fruit juice? wine?) on a saucer and a cup (bowl), similar to our own, set on our left. There is a flowered pot, an elaborate china container (sugar bowl?), a full pitcher of cream (we look down into it), a green-sided box, two plates of fruit, a basket of bread. All these things are flooded from behind with daylight. They cast shadows of unequal degree toward us. We feel the light on our body, face.

From the mysterious design of the wallpaper—latticework against strong magenta which stops halfway up to give way to smoky blue with a decorative pattern of flowers—a figure emerges on the left. A third of her is off the canvas and only part of her right hand can be seen holding a glass. Most baffling of all is a brown and orange mass to our right. It could be an elbow and a puffed sleeve or a chair with a pillow or, as some claim, a face.

This mysteriousness is partly brought about by the absence of sufficient "information." Other mysteries are created through the purposeful denial of what we know by what we are shown. For example: in the painting *Le Petit Déjeuner* (c.1930) Mme. Bonnard is shown nearly hunched over a table. We are so close that we are in danger of falling toward her. She is eating something with a spoon. Her left hand is steadying the bowl. This hand is a mere paddle coming from a ridiculous wrist and without noticeable fingers. All is obscured by a coffee pot that sways to the left like something made from brown jelly. A large yellow-ochre jug dominates the foreground. It too sways but is held in check by the luminous patch of blues at the upper right of the canvas. Everything appears to be placed on a cloth-covered tray—there is a nice treatment of folds at its corner—but the cup and saucer immediately before us haven't been given enough room in which to exist. We know hands have fingers. We know ceramic containers don't sway about. Here our eyes tell us otherwise. It is not even clear whether the pretty lavender and yellow tablecloth is supposed to fall straight down, dropping from the foreground edge of the table *directly* beneath the edge of the tray, or is willfully misdrawn, which the diagonal line continuing from the corner of the tray to the right-hand corner of the picture would suggest in terms of normal perspective. Thus irrational spatial placement is added to ambiguity of

33

forms. So is manipulation of the field of vision. Bonnard often painted things as though seen through a wide-angle lens. He used the phenomenon of peripheral vision for both formal and emotional purposes—the clearer the focus the greater the immediacy, reticence is expressed by blurring.

The rooms Bonnard painted were very often not even his. They belonged to hotels or briefly rented houses. The objects, therefore, were not always his. But Bonnard traveled with a whole suite of luggage packed by the mind's eye, always in his possession, and was able that way to lay claim to any area no matter how impersonal, foreign or strange. Through selection, observation and love, he transformed ordinary, even banal objects into things of beauty, even distinction. Through him the commonplace breakfast table became exotic. He once remarked marvelously that peaches "sometimes resemble a setting sun; only it's a sunset that does not disappear," adding with typical irony, "which is most convenient for a painter."

All, anatomy and identity, give way to the primacy of color. It is with dabs, "petals" of color, that Bonnard "floats" his images onto canvas. And his concentration, in terms of color, was prodigious. He was noted for being able to paint a number of highly complex pictures on canvases tacked to wildly active wallpaper. His colors were *remembered* colors. Colors loved and collected. Colors studied over a cup of coffee.

OPPOSITE: *Bonnard's portrait of his wife at breakfast,* Le Petit Déjeuner. *Among the familiar family objects, an oft-painted brown coffee pot.*

LEFT: Le Café: *the artist's wife enjoying a cup of morning coffee in the company of their dog.*

On Stage

Because the theater is live and life-size it would seem a perfect place to stage a breakfast. And, to tell the truth, it sometimes has been. But the most successful dramatic meals have tended to be more *public* ones: meals involving outsiders like luncheons, teas and, most especially, dinner parties. As these functions have a lot in common with theater they fit well into dramatic forms. The people depicted have dressed and prepared themselves to be seen and have decided on the roles they are to play and the reactions they hope to evoke.

An exception to this is, of course, romantic comedy, a preeminent example of which is Noel Coward's *Private Lives* in which intimacy, charged with sexual innuendo, is given full play in the last act, the morning after. After *what* is part of the fun. This unpublic face made public creates a delicious sense of eavesdropping in the audience, appealing to the baser Peeping Tom in us all.

The plot is far too intricate to outline here. Let me just explain that Amanda and Elyot are divorced, they have re-met while on honeymoon with their new spouses, Victor and Sibyl respectively, and they have fallen back in love with one another. In the last act we find Victor and Sibyl in love as well and Amanda and Elyot recovering from a terrific, funny drunken fight the night before. Coward has skillfully managed to get them all together in various degrees of disarray, outrage, embarrassment and huff. Amanda, ever super-stylish (her part was created by

the incomparable Gertrude Lawrence), has just decided that if she is going to have to stay and discuss the situation she might as well order some coffee.

The sparring continues. Amanda serves everyone except Elyot and when he says that he would like some coffee she passes the pot and the milk to him. He then pours it himself and furiously bangs the pot down causing the others to start. Then, to Amanda's "Brioche?", Victor jumps. They are all a bit nervy. Elyot, who of course hasn't been asked, says he would like one, "And some butter, and some jam," and helps himself. They all discuss the merits and faults of the South of France in summer. Conversation begins to languish. Then a verbal duel begins between Victor and Sibyl. Throughout this duel Amanda and Elyot continue to eat and drink like conspirators, winking and smiling at one another and passing things. As the duel turns into a full-scale quarrel Amanda and Elyot "laugh silently." He takes her hand and kisses it. Then they kiss. Then he whispers something to her with which she nods in agreement. They both rise quietly, pick up their suitcases, hats and gloves, and, as Sibyl slaps Victor's face and he shakes her hard by the shoulders, Amanda and Elyot go "smilingly out through the double doors and ——." The curtain falls.

Harold Pinter's world is altogether different. From the grubby household of *The Birthday Party* to the expensive townhouse of *No Man's Land* an air of abstract menace fills the stage. We never quite know where we are or who the people we're watching with such fascination are. They tell us things. They tell one another things. But the things are often unconnected or contradictory. In *No Man's Land* (unforgettably first performed, especially by John Gielgud playing Spooner, the seedy poet, and Ralph Richardson as the successful author Hirst), Foster, who *appears* to be a sort of companion/housekeeper to Hirst in whose house the action takes place (although on entering he has claimed to be Hirst's son), says near the end of the first act, "Have you ever met your host? He's my father . . . He was going to stay at home, listen to some lieder . . . Who are you, by the way?" To which Spooner, who has been rattling on for some time and drinking with Hirst, replies, "I'm a friend of his." This leads to a sarcastic speech by Foster when Briggs—who appears to be a kind of butler/thug—comes in: he introduces Spooner to Briggs as "Mr. Friend." Hirst, who earlier went off to try to sleep, returns to ask who Spooner is. Foster answers that he says he's a friend of Hirst's. Later, quite out of the blue, Hirst says to Spooner, "I know you from somewhere." A bit later Foster announces to Hirst: "I must clean the house. No one else'll do

Intimacy charged with sexual innuendo, the breakfast scene in Noel Coward's Private Lives.

it. Your financial adviser is coming to breakfast. I've got to think about that. His taste changes from day to day. One day he wants boiled eggs and toast, the next day orange juice and poached eggs, the next scrambled eggs and smoked salmon, the next mushroom omelette and champagne. Your financial adviser's dreaming of his breakfast. He's dreaming of eggs. Eggs, eggs. What kind of eggs? I'm exhausted . . ."

The second act takes place the following morning. Spooner is alone in the room. The curtains are closed. Spooner tries the door. It is locked. He sits shivering. He hears the door being unlocked and Briggs comes in. He opens the curtains to the daylight and asks if Spooner is hungry. Spooner replies, "Food? I never touch it." Briggs tells him the financial adviser hasn't turned up and that he can have his breakfast. He indirectly repeats his offer: "I won't bring you breakfast if you're going to waste it." To which Spooner rejoins, "I abhor waste."

When Briggs returns with a tray it has breakfast dishes on it covered by silver lids and a bottle of champagne in an ice bucket. "Scrambled eggs," he states, and asks if he should open the champagne. Spooner answers yes and looks under the various lids. He butters some toast. As he eats, Briggs draws up a chair and sits, watching. Then he launches into a long story about how he first met Foster and about the intricacies of the one-way street system leading to Bolsover Street—"The one trouble was that,

once in, you couldn't get out"—and at the end he asks, "When did you last have champagne for breakfast?" Spooner answers that "to be quite honest" he's a champagne drinker, that he knows a great deal about wines, having made many trips to Dijon in the thirties with his French translator, and that what his translator translated was his verse. He is a poet. Briggs orders him to finish up the bottle. Spooner asks him why he was locked in the room. Briggs tells him to let him know when he's ready for coffee. Spooner says he must be off as he has a meeting at twelve, and thanks him for the breakfast. Later, when Hirst enters, he cordially addresses Spooner as "Charles." He then asks "Denson"—Briggs—for coffee. he goes into a wild reminiscence of the last time he saw Spooner back in "'38 at the club" and of how he seduced Spooner's wife Emily—"I was an integral part of her shopping expedition."

This all but surreal conversation continues throughout the act and climaxes when Spooner attempts to join the household—"Let me live with you and be your secretary"—and has a marvelous long monologue about all his qualifications which includes an offer to do a poetry reading at the Bull's Head.

The play ends with Spooner saying, "You are in no man's land. Which never moves, which never changes, which never grows older, but which remains forever, icy and silent." There is a silence.

Hirst says, "I'll drink to that" and the light slowly fades.

Terence Rattigan is another master of the modern theater, but a quite different kind of writer from Pinter. In their writing his plays are quite straight forward. He saves them from a danger of too much sentiment through a counterpoint of the matter-of-fact.

In the second play of his hotel duet *Separate Tables*—"Table Number Seven" (a typical Rattigan alienating device—the playwright is talking about people not furniture)—the *idea* of breakfast, of there being one for the protagonist at that table, in that very room, among those same people, comes as a kind of bell of benediction. Of course there has been a scandal and an attempt to oust a man. And there is a shy, nervous woman who cares about him. He cares for her too. But in order to be able to stay on, the man has to stop lying about himself which he has been doing for years. Then, with everyone expecting him *not* to appear for dinner, he suddenly does and one by one the other guests "forgive" him by means of various forms of polite acknowledgment. All except the shy woman's mother who had instigated the effort for his removal.

A scene from "Table Number Seven," part of Terence Rattigan's hotel duet Separate Tables.

The play ends as follows: The room is empty now except for the "casual" couple (as opposed to "regular"), the man, the shy woman and the serving girl Doreen who has just finished serving the man. It is she who introduces the idea of the future.

Doreen: . . . Now what about breakfast?
Major [He isn't. That's one of his lies]: Breakfast?
Doreen: Joe got it wrong about you going, didn't he? (There is a pause. Sibyl looks steadily at the Major, who now raises his eyes from his plate and meets her glance.)
Major: (quietly) Yes, he did.
Doreen: That's good. Breakfast usual time, then?
Major: Yes, Doreen. Breakfast usual time.
Doreen exits. The four people continue eating in silence.

None of these plays has had very much to do with actual food: too messy to deal with, too liable to slow down the action. My last example is a famous play in which even the props are gone. You might think of it as an invisible breakfast so vividly evoked that we can almost smell and taste it.

The play in question is Thorton Wilder's *Our Town*. In the 1939 Acting Edition of his play, Wilder writes this simple descriptive sentence: "You arrive at breakfast time and are carried through one entire day in the lives of these good people." And it's true. What better way than to begin at the beginning and follow along from there. The second act is described, somewhat disarmingly, as "culminating in a moving wedding scene which contains all those elements of poignant sorrow and abundant happiness that make for solemnity and impressiveness." The play closes with an unforgettable scene in the cemetery and a return to morning—the morning of February 11, 1899: Emily's twelfth birthday. Emily has died but she's been granted her wish to return. She learns through this experience that there is no return, ever. As she watches the town of her childhood wake and her family getting ready for the new day she remains unseen by them all. Her mother calls her, stokes the stove, greets the milkman Mr. Newsome, comments on the weather (it's cold, less than "ten below"). Emily talks to her mother who responds as though her daughter is upstairs. Her father comes home from a speech-giving expedition to a college. Emily tries to enter into the gone world of the past but breaks down. She goes completely unnoticed by her mother who remains unaware that this is the future as well as the present and that her daughter is twenty-six and dead. She admonishes that birthday or no birthday she wants Emily to eat her breakfast "good and slow" so that she will "grow up and be a good strong girl." She tells her to chew her bacon "good and slow" so that it will help to keep her "warm on a cold day." Emily bursts into tears, crying out that she didn't *realize* "all that was going on and we never noticed!"

Wilder wants the audience to realize that Emily is under strong emotion, but that it is the emotion of wonder rather than sadness, that there is realization along with poignancy. He feels it is important for the performers to maintain a "dryness of tone" and a "shyness of emotion." He writes of a "scorn of verisimilitude" and thinks it advisable for the actors to perform much of the business of preparing breakfast with their backs to the audience so as not to "distract and provoke its attention with too distinct and perhaps puzzling a picture of the many operations of coffee grinding, porridge stirring, etc."

We reach the point where the morning papers are about to be delivered. The 5:45 train from Boston is about to be flagged. A train whistle sounds offstage: profound music of nostalgia. "Naturally out in the country, all around, there've been lights on for some time, what with milkin' and so on." "But town folks sleep late"—a lovely bit of Wilder spoof, we have just been told it's not yet 6 A.M. The Gibbs' home begins to come alive. Mrs. Gibbs comes downstairs. She raises a shade, opens a window, begins to build a wood fire in the stove. All imagined events. Right from the start Time is bent and reworked.

Mrs. Gibbs grinds imaginary coffee into an imaginary pot on an imaginary stove.

And so it goes. Mrs. Webb comes down *her* stairs and begins preparing breakfast in counterpoint to Mrs. Gibbs' actions. The paper boy materializes and it is he who is the first character to speak. He calls "Mornin', Doc!" to Doc Gibbs. Mrs. Webb puts bacon on the skillet. Stretch of dialogue. Mrs. Webb puts coffee on. Dialogue. Mrs. Gibbs cuts bread then a pie. Mrs. Webb rolls out biscuits. The Stage Manager talks about the paper boy. Mrs. Gibbs spreads a table cloth, gets a cup and spoon from the cupboard. She crosses to stove, turns bacon, breaks four eggs into skillet. The milkman arrives. There is a friendly exchange between him and Mrs. Gibbs. She calls to the children to get up. Mrs. Webb puts biscuits in the oven and sets the table. Doc Gibbs enters and is told to sit down and drink his coffee. This counterpoint of action between the two households continues under the dialogue throughout the act and we learn more and more about the two families whose children are to fall in love and marry in the second act. All the intimacy between husband and wife, parents and children, is skillfully revealed. Along the way oatmeal is served; classic American admonitions are sounded: "Now I won't have it. Breakfast is just as good as any other meal and I won't have you gobblin' like wolves. It'll stunt your growth, that's a fact . . ."; "You know the rules as well as I do—no books at table. As for me, I'd rather have my children healthy than bright." To which her daughter smartly replies that she's both— only to be countered by a terse "Eat your breakfast."

Meanwhile, over at the Gibbs' place Rebecca has just made the comically shocking statement that she loves money most in the world. To which her mother gives exactly the same reply as Mrs. Webb—"Eat your breakfast."

The school bell is heard in the distance and the four children rush out, meet. The girls pair off as do the boys and they exit "chatting gaily."

The two mothers clear up and begin their chores. Mrs. Gibbs feeds the chickens and Mrs. Webb begins stringing beans. Mrs. Gibbs offers to help her and the two mothers begin to talk.

A far different, earlier life, in another country, is shown in Thomas Dekker's hearty and vivid picture of sixteenth-century London, *The Shoemaker's Holiday*. In the third scene of the first act Simon Eyre, the shoemaker of the title, admonishes everyone to clean up after breakfast: "Where be these boys, these girls, these drabs, these scoundrels? They wallow in the fat brewiss [bread soaked in pot liquor] of my bounty, and lick the crumbs of my table, yet will not rise to see my walks cleansed. Come out you powder-beef queens! ...."

He goes on to hire Sir Hugh Lacy, Earl of Lincoln, who is disguised as a Dutch shoemaker. One of Eyre's workers makes fun of Sir Hugh's speech [made-up Dutch] and talks of food and privilege: "Yaw, yaw! He speaks like a jackdaw that gapes to be fed with cheese-curds. Oh, he'll give a

villainous pull at a can of double-beer, but Hodge and I have the vantage, we must drink first because we are the eldest journeymen."

Eyre welcomes the newcomer and instructs his wife to "bid your maids, your trillibubs [slatterns, sluts] make ready my fine men's breakfasts."

In the second scene of the fourth act, two of Eyre's workers have this exchange:

Hodge: Go, Hans, make haste again. Come, who lacks work?
Firk: I, master, for I lack my breakfast; tis munching-time and past.
Hodge: Is't so? Why, then leave work, Ralph. To breakfast! Boy, look to the tools. Come, Ralph; Come, Firk.

In the next act Firk remarks to Ralph who has come upon an important discovery: "'Snails [God's nails], Ralph, thou has lost thy part of three pots, a country man gave me to breakfast." And in scene two of the fifth act the shoemakers are found celebrating Shrove Tuesday:

All: The pancake-bell rings, the pancake bell! Trilill my hearts!
Firk: Oh brave! Oh sweet bell! O delicate pancakes! Open the doors, my hearts, and shut up the windows! keep in the house, let out the pancakes! Oh rare, my hearts! Let's march

together for the honour of Saint Hugh to the great new hall in Gracious Streetcorner, which our master, the new lord mayor, hath built.
Ralph : O the crew of good fellows that will dine at my lord mayor's cost today! ...
Firk : O musical bell, still! O Hodge, O my brethren! There's cheer for the heavens: venison-pasties walk up and down piping hot, like sergeants; beef and brewiss comes marching in dry-vats; fritters and pancakes comes trowling in in wheel-barrows; hens and oranges hopping in porters'-baskets; collops [bacon] and eggs in scuttles; and tarts and custards comes quavering in in malt-shovels.

Enter more Prentices

All : Whoop, look here, look here!
Hodge : How now, mad lads, whither away so fast?
First Prentice : Whither? Why, to the great new hall, know you not why? The lord mayor hath bidden all the prentices in London to breakfast this morning ...

And the play comes to a close with Eyre, the Lord Mayor, asking the King to partake of his breakfast feast:

Eyre : Vouchsafe to taste of a poor banquet that stands sweetly waiting for your sweet presence.
King : I shall undo thee, Eyre, only with feasts. Already have I been too troublesome? Say, have I not?
Eyre : O my dear king, Sim Eyre was taken unawares upon a day of shroving, which I promised long ago to the prentices of London. For, an't please your highness, in time past, I bare the water tankard, and my coat Sits not a whit the worse upon my back; And them, upon a morning, some mad boys, It was Shrove Tuesday, even as 'tis now, Gave me my breakfast, and I swore then by the stopple of my tankard, if ever I came to be lord mayor of London, I would feast all the prentices. This day, my liege, I did it, and the slaves had an hundred tables five times covered; they are gone home and vanished; Yet add more honour to the gentle trade, Taste of Eyre's banquet, Simon's happy made.
King : Eyre, I will taste of thy banquet, and will say,
I have not met more pleasure on a day.
Friends of the gentle craft, thanks to you all,
Thanks, my kind lady mayoress, for our cheer.
Come, lords, a while let's revel it at home!
When all our sports and banquetings are done,
Wars must right wrongs which Frenchmen have begun.

43

Victoriana

The world of wealth, leisure, large houses and lots of servants, of the display of possessions and the pursuit of pleasure that flourished in nineteenth-century Britain, indulged in eating habits quite different from the generally unimaginative and meager meals characteristic of recent years. An anonymous work published in 1882 entitled PARTY-GIVING ON EVERY SCALE *describes a number of lavish and specialized breakfasts. Here are three that the Victorians especially delighted in, as presented in that book.*

Bachelors' Breakfasts—Bachelors' breakfast parties are usually given from 11 to 12, and expense is a secondary consideration with these hosts, if a consideration at all—to have every thing earliest in season is the prevailing idea. Lamb cutlets or lamb chops . . . broiled salmon . . . oysters . . . plovers' eggs . . . spring chickens . . . whitebait . . . *pâté de foie gras*, at 2 guineas the *pâté*, and so on.

At these breakfasts good claret is generally given rather than champagne, in addition to tea, coffee, and liqueurs. Champagne is principally given by young men who have not learnt to appreciate good claret.

Wedding Breakfasts—The orthodox "Wedding Breakfast" might more properly be termed a "Wedding Luncheon," as it assumes the character of that meal to a great extent; in any case, it bears little relation to the breakfast of the day, although the title of breakfast is still applied to it, out of compliment to tradition. . . . The difference between a small wedding breakfast and a large one is rather in the number and variety of dishes than in the character of the said viands; while with regard to the display made of plate, fruit and flowers, this is necessarily regulated by the style of breakfast given and the number of guests invited. . . .

A breakfast given at an hotel or one given in furnished apartments offers little choice in the arrangements, as in either case there is but one alternative, the hotel *cuisine* or the confectioner's *cuisine*, neither of which ranks particularly high in public estimation . . . in comparison with home *cuisine*. When a breakfast is given at the home of the bride, and is not "sent in" or supplied by a confectioner, but "made at home," it is considered a very superior style of breakfast, in other words, a more fashionable one to give. But this is taking for granted that the home cook is equal to the occasion, or that the services of an experienced cook can be secured for the event . . . and as no profit is to accrue, the one object is to provide the best of its kind that can be compassed. . . .

The true art of giving a wedding breakfast is to

introduce as much variety into the menu as possible, and to tempt the appetite with light and *appétissant* delicacies, rather than to repel it by the display of a huge quantity of heavy and substantial fare.

[After talking about the cake which he refers to as that "unwholesome dainty," the author goes on to the kinds of foods most suitable. Beginning with oysters, his list includes: cold salmon; mutton or lamb cutlets; cucumbers, peas, asparagus or spinach; lobster mayonnaise ("as much a standing dish at a wedding breakfast as is the wedding cake") or lobster salad; *suprême de volaille à la crême*; plovers' eggs with aspic jelly; prawns in aspic; collared eel in aspic; *pâtés*, cold meats; partridges, quail, larks with truffles; chicken or turkey; hams; cold game-pie; lamb; pigeon pie; jellies flavored preferably with Noyeau or Maraschino liqueur (strawberries, raspberries, currants, etc., are "not *à la mode*"); creams—usually "strawberry and coffee, raspberry and Italian"; *Meringues glacés*; cakes; fruit; champagne, most of all, and sherry. The breakfast can be either stand-up or sit-down.]

The breakfast commences with one hot *entrée*, if the breakfast is a sitting-down one; it is also fashionable . . . to give one hot roast in addition to a hot *entrée*. . . . At a standing-up breakfast soup is never given; neither are hot *entreés* or hot roasts provided.

Hunt Breakfasts—A Hunt Breakfast partakes of the character of a cold luncheon on a large scale, with . . . wines and liqueurs. These breakfasts are given . . . by the master of the hounds, by the members of the hunt, or by any country gentleman near whose residence the meet takes place. . . . No invitations are issued for these breakfasts beyond those contained in the general notice given by the M.F.H. [Master of Fox Hounds] respecting the meets of the current week.

These breakfasts are given at the expense of the host of the day, and are entirely apart from the expenses of the hunt. The guests generally average 40 to 100, including members of the hunt and non-members, gentlemen and farmers, residents and strangers.

The breakfast is given in the large dining-room, great hall, or billiard-room, according to the accommodation required, one long table occupies the centre of the room. Breakfast-covers are placed the length of the table; a knife and fork and plate to each cover, and as each place is vacated a fresh cover is placed in readiness for a new comer. Ladies are seldom present at hunt breakfasts, and those who ride or drive to the meet, and are acquainted with the lady of the house, . . . are ushered on their arrival into the drawing-room or morning-room, where refreshments are offered them, tea, coffee, sherry, sandwiches, cake, etc.

9:30 to 10 is the time usually fixed for a hunt

breakfast, although this is regulated by the hour at which the hounds are to meet. At hunt breakfasts hot *entrées* are not given; a large supply of cold viands is necessary; cold beef is the *pièce de resistance* at these entertainments, as the hunting farmers prefer something substantial to commence upon.

Twenty to thirty lbs. of sirloin or corned beef is usually provided. . . . Cold roast pheasant or game pie; roast chickens or roast turkey would also be given; and as this game and poultry would be furnished from the home preserves and home farm, the cost would be considerably under market price.

A piece of cheese, weighing from 12 lbs. to 15 lbs. . . . either Cheddar or North Wiltshire . . . bread and cheese is in great demand at hunt breakfasts.

All the cold meats, game, etc., are placed on the breakfast-table, and the guests help themselves. . . . As a rule gentlemen eat but little at hunt breakfasts, and breakfast at home before starting; farmers, on the contrary, make a hearty meal, having perhaps breakfasted at a much earlier hour. A host, when ordering a hunt breakfast, takes into consideration the class of guests he expects, and regulates the supply according to the probable demand.

Sherry, brandy, cherry-brandy, liqueurs, and ale are always provided. Champagne is only occasionally given.

An eighteenth-century hunt breakfast in France matches the luxury of its later English counterpart. The painting is by J. F. de Troy.

The normal daily routine of the Victorians is described by Dorothy Hartley in Food in England *(1954).*

The Victorian breakfast was the hearty reward of early rising, and followed an hour's "office work" and family prayers. The time was usually eight o'clock. The maids rose at five-thirty (five o'clock for the kitchen maid). The daughters of the house were down by seven o'clock and did an hour's music practice, study, or brisk exercise. (In the new Methodist households, an hour's devotional study was quite usual.) The master of the house used his early hours for letters, estate work, and business affairs; the matron used hers for household affairs, and while she had a very young family she was permitted to wear a morning wrapper and spend part of this time in the nursery. The household work is that of a country house today, but with no gas or electricity, and no labour-saving appliances. The housemaid first opened the wooden shutters and windows, cleared the grates, and lit fires. She swept and dusted the breakfast-room, hall and staircases, while the other maid carried up the huge polished brass cans of boiling bath water, set down the flat tin "splash baths" from their stands against the bedroom walls, and carried jugs of scalding shaving water to the gentlemen's dressing-rooms.

In the kitchen the cook now descended, and woe betide the kitchen wench who has not a scuttle of soot to show for her cleaning of the kitchen flues!

The kitchen maid must then "do" the back door and fetch the morning's milk, collect the eggs, and wait upon the cook while she "makes the breakfast." Soon muffins are hot, toast crisp, fish cooked, bacon cut ready for grilling, plates set to heat; and, the table laid, cook, housemaid, and all the servants hurriedly put on clean aprons, wash their hands, and join the gardener and his boy, to file solemnly into the breakfast-room for family prayers. . . .

Breakfast was a "family" meal. The servants usually had theirs at the same time, so it was a point of "consideration" not to need "waiting on" during breakfast. The woman of the house made the tea, using the expensive teas kept in the beautifully made tea-caddy of the period (lined with lead foil, it had two lidded compartments for "green" or "black" teas, with a cut-glass sugar bowl between them).

The kettle boiling upon the hearth was of polished brass, with a china or glass handle, and a neat woolwork tea-kettle holder hung alongside the fireplace. Hot teacakes, breakfast rolls, or muffins were on a trivet before the fire. The boiled eggs were kept hot in a china dish—the cover shaped like a hen (some of these dishes were beautifully modelled)— or on a silver egg-stand.

After breakfast the domesticated matron usually made a small rite of "washing-up the breakfast things herself," either in an adjoining pantry, or the maid carried in a wooden bowl of hot soapy water, placed it on a japanned tea-tray on the table, with a clean cloth, and the washing-up was done "with neatness and despatch."...

The mistress herself put the china back "together with breakfast cruet and sundry etceteras," into the special china cupboard in the breakfast room.

Many "corner cupboards" of this period, now used for "show" china, were originally made for daily use.

In theory this "washing up" of the breakfast things left the maids time to go upstairs and "do" the bedrooms which, by the time they had plumped up the feather beds, emptied gallons of bath water and slops, arranged clean towels and draped the bed hangings, kept them busy till ten o'clock.

Cook, too, scurried around, and by nine o'clock was waiting respectfully to receive her mistress in consultation over the day's meals....

The proper way to lay a breakfast table in England in the 1890s, according to the redoubtable Mrs. Beeton.

Cereal

> Have you tried Wheaties?
> They're the whole wheat with all of the bran.
> Won't you try Wheaties?
> For wheat is the best food of man!
>
> *First singing radio commercial (1926)*

> "A lot of air has been sold in packaged foods, and cornflakes have been described as a great way to make air stand up."
>
> *Richard Mackarness in*
> Eat Fat and Grow Slim *(1975)*

Cereal comes from the Roman goddess of grain, Ceres. Festivals called *cerealia* were held in her honor around 500 B.C.

It is claimed that 50 percent of American families eat cereals regularly, 90 percent at least once in a while. More than 75,000,000 servings are consumed every day. No wonder there are hundreds of cereals available on the market and eaten all over the world. Both Australia and Canada exceed the United States in per capita consumption. Battle Creek, Michigan, accounts for the production of two-thirds of all ready-to-eat cereals in the United States—700,000,000 pounds a year.

Cooked cereal porridge has been around for some time. During the middle of the nineteenth century Scottish oatmeal became popular in the U.S. Then rolled oats—rather than ground—were developed and at first only sold as a health food in drug stores. The product was thought suitable for children, invalids, and people descended from Scots. But slowly it spread to the grocery stores and interest was aroused as to the possibility of cracked or rolled *wheat*. This led to four major discoveries which made commercial exploitation of ready-to-eat cereals possible.

In 1893 Henry D. Perkey of Denver, Colorado, produced a shredded wheat. He had supposedly encountered a man in a Nebraska town suffering from indigestion who experienced relief by breakfasting on boiled wheat and milk. Mr. Perkey, who also suffered from indigestion, found that the unfamiliar food worked for him. First he developed, with his brother, a shredding machine, thinking that people would buy it and shred their own wheat. But as most people had never tasted the stuff they showed little interest in a machine to make it. So Perkey and his brother developed the now famous Shredded Wheat Biscuit (bought by Nabisco in 1928). Publicity always helps and Perkey exploited the location of his Shredded Wheat Bakery at Niagara Falls, New York, opening his premises to thousands of visitors to the Falls and letting them spread the word.

Dr. John Kellogg and his brother W. K. Kellogg came up with the first flaked wheat product in 1894.

Again initially thought of as a health food, it was served at the Battle Creek Sanitarium and sold to vegetarians and health food advocates. In the 1860s Seventh Day Adventists had established a medical boarding house in Battle Creek to work on dietary problems for health as well as spiritual reasons. They believed people should abstain from eating meats and using alcohol, tobacco, tea, coffee or patent medicines. Dr. Kellogg turned the boarding-house into an institution of world renown. In the 1920s the staff numbered 1,800 and patients and guests about 1,500. Among those who attended it for special diets and treatment were William Jennings Bryan, Admiral Richard E. Byrd, Harvey Firestone, John D. Rockefeller, Jr., J. C. Penny, Robert La Follette, Eddie Cantor, Johnny Weismuller, Amelia Earhart, H. G. Wells, Herbert Hoover, Carrie Nation, Henry Ford, George Bernard Shaw, the merchant tycoons Kress and Kresge, movie stars, dictators and nobility.

In the process of his association with the sanitarium, the doctor invented some eighty new grain and nut products. They were not developed commercially, however, until Dr. Kellogg's brother and C. W. Post began their campaigns.

By the turn of the century Battle Creek was like a gold-rush town and the cereal boom had produced products with names like Tryachewa, Oatsina, Malta Vita and Tryabita. More than forty food companies were started in the early 1900s with more than a hundred brands of corn flakes and over forty brands of wheat flakes going out to grocers. The first *puffed* cereal appeared in 1902 and was the discovery of Alexander Anderson.

Charles W. Post was to become the wealthiest cereal producer of them all. He had a gift for selling and was an inventive man. He had originally come to Battle Creek for his health and so knew what the needs were. Investing $46.85 in equipment and $21.91 in materials, he developed a hot cereal beverage in 1894 which he called Monk's Brew and later Postum. Through advertising he was able to sell enough of his new drink to make a net profit within two years. (In fact, he is often referred to as the "father of modern advertising.") But Postum was a seasonal seller and Post had to find something to balance out his production schedule. In 1897 he came up with Grape Nuts. In 1904 he added Elijah's Manna, but the public objected to such biblical references and he had to change it to Post Toasties. In ten years he had become a multimillionaire.

W. K. Kellogg was no slouch either when it came to promoting a product. It was his idea to put his signature on every package as this seemed to suggest a personal commitment and responsibility. He employed contests, premiums, cut-outs, games and package inserts, and they all worked.

These companies along with the producers of Ralston Cream of Wheat, Quaker Oats, Wheaties and others had, in effect, invented a new class of

51

Happy Children

"Children are Love's flowers to brighten the world." Let them be kindly nourished.

Quaker Oats contains every food element required to perfectly nourish children during the period of rapid growth. It gives them strong, lithe bodies, clear eyes, good teeth and rosy cheeks.

THE EASY FOOD

Quaker Oats

THE WORLD'S BREAKFAST

ACCEPT NO SUBSTITUTE

Nourishment and convenience are the emphasis in this early advertisement (1899) for Quaker Oats.

foods—something easily storeable and transportable. They had also changed a nation's eating habits, begun to make people more conscious of nutrition, and helped to inaugurate the era of "convenience foods."

The role accident often plays in the history of discovery is reasserted by the way in which Wheaties evolved. It seems a man in a Minneapolis health clinic in the 1920s was feeding bran as a bulk food to his overweight patients. One morning he stirred the bran too vigorously and some of it splashed onto the hot stove. Thin wafers formed and came off quite easily. The man tasted them and found they were crisp and tasty. He contacted the president of the Washburn Crosby Company and an agreement resulted to work on a process to manufacture the new food. The work continued for several years without success until the head miller decided to switch to wheat. He tried thirty-six varieties and finally found one that worked. A name was found for it by a clever woman named Jane Bausman, who realized that people like diminutives such as "Teddy" or "sweetie" or "movies"—and so "Wheaties" was born, the Breakfast of Champions.

A lot has happened since then. We now have Cheerios and Corn Kix, Total and Country Corn, Buc-Wheats and Pep and Concentrates, Wheat Chex, Wheatena and Cap'n Crunch, Corn Flakes and Country Morning, Rice Krispies (which go "Snap! Crackle! Pop!"), Product 19 and Special K,

among countless others; we have fortified cereals sprayed with vitamins. In some of the newer "natural" products like Alpen and Granola, things like cinnamon and fruit, nuts, coconut and honey have been introduced. And nowadays even hot cereals take only five to fifteen minutes to cook, and can be kept hot in a double boiler over a low heat.

All very well and good, but the argument about cereals rages around what happens to them during processing. Cereal grain is a seed and is made up of the germ, the endosperm and the bran. The germ is the center of the seed and contains the highest-quality protein, the B vitamin thiamine and several other elements. The endosperm is where food for the germinating plant is reserved. It is composed chiefly of carbohydrates—the plant's source of energy. The bran is the seed's protective coating and contains carbohydrates, iron and B vitamins along with protein and phosphorus. Various processes in manufacturing effect these three elements and, for example, the reintroduction of lost vitamins or protein brings about a different result than if they were retained in the first place. Therefore the differences between manufacturers who opt for "fortification" and "enrichment," claiming these improve their product and those who insist on whole-grain products.

At no point is it simple to determine the nutrient value of cereal products. The relationship between calories and protein is typical of the dilemma.

According to information supplied by the manufacturers, a cereal like Special K contains 6 grams of protein and 100 calories in a $1\frac{1}{4}$ cup serving, while the same amount of Wheaties contains 2.5 grams of protein and 101 calories. And when you take into consideration the calorie-protein content of various toppings, you need a computer to work out just what nutrients you're getting! One teaspoon of sugar contains 17 calories and no protein. One teaspoon of honey contains 21 calories and no protein. One-quarter of a cup of Half & Half supplies 80 calories and 1.9 grams of protein as compared with an equal amount of skim milk which comes to 22 calories and 2.2 grams of protein.

And as for amino acids, it turns out that cereal really gives excellent protein value only when combined with other foods such as milk, cheese, eggs, wheat germ, and brewer's yeast.

A contemporary cereal package from Post, designed to show all the goodies within (by courtesy of the manufacturers).

Post

C.W. Post™

FAMILY STYLE CEREAL
WITH RAISINS

OATS

BROWN SUGAR

RICE

WHEAT

RAISINS

COCONUT

ALMONDS

HONEY

K

NET WT. 15 OZ.   FORTIFIED·8 ESSENTIAL VITAMINS

Okie's Breakfast

John Steinbeck wrote a lyrical description of migrant workers breakfasting as a working note for THE GRAPES OF WRATH, *his classic study of "Okies" in California during the thirties. It was not used in the novel but was included in* THE PORTABLE JOHN STEINBECK, *where it was called simply "Breakfast."*

This thing fills me with pleasure. I don't know why, I can see it in the smallest detail. I find myself recalling it again and again, each time bringing more detail out of a sunken memory, remembering brings the curious warm pleasure.

It was very early in the morning. The eastern mountains were black-blue, but behind them the light stood up faintly colored at the mountain rims with a washed red, growing colder, grayer and darker as it went up and overhead until, at a place near the west, it merged with pure light.

And it was cold, not painfully so, but cold enough so that I rubbed my hands and shoved them deep into my pockets, and I hunched my shoulders up and scuffled my feet on the ground. Down in the valley where I was, the earth was that lavender gray of dawn. I walked along a country road and ahead of me I saw a tent that was only a little lighter gray than the ground. Beside the tent there was a flash of orange fire seeping out of the cracks of an old rusty iron stove. Gray smoke spurted up out of the stubby stovepipe, spurted up a long way before it spread out and dissipated.

I saw a young woman beside the stove, really a girl. She was dressed in a faded cotton skirt and waist. As I came close I saw that she carried a baby in a crooked arm and the baby was nursing, its head under her waist out of the cold. The mother moved about, poking the fire, shifting the rusty lids of the stove to make a greater draft, opening the oven door; and all the time the baby was nursing. . . .

I was close now and I could smell frying bacon and baking bread, the warmest, pleasantest odors I know. From the east the light grew swiftly. I came near to the stove and stretched my hands out to it and shivered all over when the warmth struck me. Then the tent flap jerked up and a young man came out and an older man followed him. . . .

The younger had a dark stubble beard and the older had a gray stubble beard. Their heads and faces were wet, their hair dripped with water, and water stood out on their stiff beards and their cheeks shone with water. Together they stood looking quietly at the lightening east; they yawned together and looked at the light on the hill rims. They turned and saw me.

"Morning, sir," I said.

"Morning," said the young man.

The water was slowly drying on their faces. They came to the stove and warmed their hands at it.

The girl kept to her work, her face averted and her eyes on what she was doing. Her hair was tied back out of her eyes with a string and it hung down her back and swayed as she worked. She set tin cups on a big packing box, set tin plates and knives and forks out too. Then she scooped fried bacon out of the deep grease and laid it on a big tin platter, and the bacon cricked and rustled as it grew crisp. She opened the rusty door and took out a square pan full of high big biscuits.

When the smell of that hot bread came out, both of the men inhaled deeply. The young man said softly, "Keerist!"

The elder man turned to me. "Had your breakfast?"

"No."

"Well, sit down with us, then."

That was the signal. We went to the packing case and squatted on the ground about it. The young man asked, "Picking cotton?"

"No."

"We had twelve days' work so far," the young man said. . . .

The girl set out the platter of bacon, the brown high biscuits, a bowl of bacon gravy and a pot of coffee, and then she squatted down by the box too. The baby was still nursing, its head up under her waist out of the cold. . . .

We filled our plates, poured bacon gravy over our biscuits and sugared our coffee. The older man filled his mouth full and he chewed and chewed and swallowed. Then he said, "God almighty, it's good," and he filled his mouth again. . . .

We all ate quickly, frantically, and refilled our plates and ate quickly again until we were full and warm. The hot bitter coffee scalded our throats. We threw the last little bit with the grounds in it on the earth and refilled our cups.

There was color in the light now, a reddish gleam that made the air seem colder. The two men faced the east and their faces were lighted by the dawn, and I looked up for a moment and saw the image of the mountain and the light coming over it reflected in the older man's eyes.

Then the two men threw the grounds from their cups on the earth and they stood up together. "Got to get going," the older man said.

The younger turned to me. "'Fyou want to pick cotton, we could maybe get you on."

"No. I got to go along. Thanks for the breakfast."

The older man waved his hand in a negative. "O.K. Glad to have you." They walked away together. The air was blazing away down the country road.

That's all. I know, of course, some of the reasons why it was pleasant. But there was some element of great beauty there that makes the rush of warmth when I think of it.

Worldwide

Smoke-flavored trout or bannocks eaten beside a stream in the high country of the Canadian Rockies. Hot bread with butter and rose jam, a sip of sweet tea, in Turkish Bodrum with the cries of the muezzin coming from a mosque beside the sea, fishing boats returning. In Spain, a change from the usual roll and coffee: a pony of anise liqueur along with a cup of chocolate. A Cantonese starting in on slices of raw fish in a rice gruel accompanied by fried bread. In California Gold Rush country, glasses of champagne or Ramos Fizzes raised to the morning—followed by an omelette Bernaise or a steak. A meal at daybreak of mackerel and pollack caught in the clear turquoise waters off the island of Scarp in the Outer Hebrides. Boned duck's feet and tea in Hong Kong. A fisherman in Portugal tossing off some white rum and coffee along with a chunk of fresh bread. Whole heads of garlic roasted until sweet, eaten with bread by an Italian farmer. In the Danish countryside, porridge, pickled herring with onions, dark rye bread, Samsoe cheese, enjoyed in the morning light. Waking with a glass of water-clear alcohol in a mountain village in Crete, following with coffee, fat fresh goat's milk, brown bread, Mizithra cheese and gold-green thyme honey. Argentine gauchos eating meat and bread, washing it down with tea-like *yerba maté*. Dutch children sprinkling chocolate on their bread and butter while their parents eat Edam or Gouda cheese, crisp Holland rusks, sliced tomatoes with bread and butter. At an alpine inn, *Birchermuesli*, a Swiss dish involving apples, lemons, oranges, bananas, nuts, cream, brown sugar and wheat germ taken with bread and coffee. Cold toast and hot tomatoes in England or perhaps, in some country house, lambs' kidneys stewed in sherry and stock or slow-roasted partridges covered with fresh butter and mushrooms. Soft-boiled eggs in Russia, a mixture of breads, masses of tea. "Ham and haddie" in Scotland—kippers and ham with scrambled or poached eggs or whipped cream! Blueberry pancakes in a coffee shop off Sunset Boulevard in Los Angeles. Flapjacks in the sunshine overlooking Long Island Sound. . . .

To think of a place is to think of a day and a day has to have a beginning. And that beginning is associated for most of us with breakfast. So that all the places combined with all the breakfasts add up to a wide variety of food—the food of the various corners of the world.

The first meal of the day in Spain is called *desayuno* and usually consists of coffee or chocolate, rolls and jam and a crisp hot pastry called *churro* which is cooked in boiling olive oil. You can buy one at a stand and carry it away in a greasy brown bag to the nearest café to eat with bowls of half coffee/half chocolate with goat's milk. *Las onces* ("elevenses") means a stop for a grilled sausage with bread and tomatoes, some fried squid, or simply an omelette. In Galicia there is a rich almond pastry called *tarta*

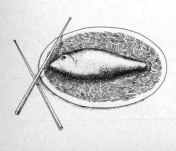

Velasquez' painting of a Spanish woman cooking eggs on an earthenware stove filled with charcoal.

de Santiago, much admired in the morning. During Holy Week in Seville you can join the locals and sip chocolate and munch *buñuelos de viento*, "fritters of air." In Valencia in the early morning, drink the juice of the superb local oranges and try a *tostada*, a pastry made of rice flour, oranges, eggs and anis.

In Portugal, hot tea is drunk with rolls, fresh butter and dark aromatic honey. In the mountains you might start with a grape peel and pip liqueur called Bogaceiro then eat a *torrados*, thick slices of bread without crusts toasted over a fire and spread with salted butter on both sides served in a napkin with black coffee. In Lisbon ordinary shops offer as many as fifteen to twenty blended coffees plus as many standard blends. You can buy coffee from Brazil, Africa, the Orient.

Catalan peasants in the Roussillon district of France breakfast on bread fresh from the baker—sometimes fried in oil or pork fat—rubbed with a piece of garlic, sprinkled with salt and a few drops of olive oil. A taste echoed by Italian children who often eat bread with oil, garlic and tomato.

In Austria during the nineteenth century a wealthy man might be served breakfast in his room at the fashionable Hotel Sacher at about nine—coffee with hot milk, crescent-shaped rolls called *Kipfel*, butter, jam and perhaps a boiled egg. Then he'd take a walk, eventually stopping at Demel's or Gerstner's or Stiebitz's for a breakfast goulash—*Frühstücksgulasch*—or some sausages. This was called *Gabelfrühstück* ("fork breakfast"). Lunch didn't happen until after one. Today the day is broken with six meals—breakfast coffee and milk and rolls (*Semmeln*), bread, butter and jam; at ten o'clock, a fork breakfast of goulash or sausages (*Wiener*, except in Vienna itself); mid-day lunch; mid-afternoon, *Jause*; a simple dinner at seven; coffee and rich cakes around eleven.

In most Latin American countries *papayas* are the everyday breakfast fruit. They are eaten plain with salt, pepper and lime. In Mexico *tortillas*, a corn-derived round flatbread is eaten with country eggs (*huevos rancheros*) with slices of avocado and a hot sauce of tomatoes and chili peppers and hot foaming chocolate. Montezuma drank his chocolate from a golden cup. An astonished Spanish friar, Bernardino de Sahagún, who accompanied the conquering Cortéz, wrote about it: "The ruler was served his chocolate, with which he finished his meal; green, made of tender cacao; honeyed chocolate made with ground-up dried flowers and green vanilla pods; bright-red chocolate; orange-colored chocolate; rose-colored chocolate; black chocolate; white chocolate . . ." (One wonders how those various colors were achieved.) Today, Mexicans who can afford it eat four meals a day. Breakfast normally consists of fruit, bread, sweet rolls, eggs and/or meat, coffee or chocolate with milk. Pineapple, oranges and other citrus fruits are popular. Breakfast oranges are often peeled so that foreigners won't be

*Mexican women preparing
tortillas, an illustration from the
French publication* Magasin
Pittoresque *(1854).*

upset by the natural green skins!

In one of the markets in Peru a traveler might try a hot boiled potato with *aji*—a chili-like mixture—or herbs and spices. *Anticuchos* are the Peruvian hot dogs. Pieces of charcoal-broiled ox heart marinated in spiced vinegar are skewered on sharpened cane and brushed with a hot sauce of oil, *aji* and spices. A drink widely imbibed in Uruguay, Paraguay, Argentina and parts of Chile and Brazil is *yerba maté*, made from the dried leaves of a shrub of the holly family. It is drunk hot or cold. The tea-like leaves are put into small, beautifully decorated gourds, boiling water added and the liquid is allowed to steep. Then it is drunk through a kind of straw—a wooden or metal tube with a perforated spoon-like strainer at the lower end. Sugar and cream are sometimes added. There is a marvelous turnover in Argentina called an *emapanadas* which is filled with chopped meat, raisins, olives and onions which could make a delicious breakfast. Like the American cowboys the Latin American gauchos eat meat mostly—beef or sheep depending on the location.

Anthony Trollope, visiting Jamaica in 1859, complained that his host sneered at the local recipes and foods he longed to try, feeding him instead on canned meats and vegetables and steak with onions for breakfast. He concluded that it was "sheer snobbery" that nothing was considered valuable by the colonials unless it came from Europe. In contrast, the London *Times'* "Good Food Guide" (April 17, 1976) reported that "Sunday morning breakfast at the Casa Monte Hotel is a comparatively cheap way to encounter local food. [It] is up in the hilly green-swamped part of Kingston, and the variety is as all-enveloping as the view. Traditionalists can stay with bacon, sausages and scrambled eggs. More questing appetites can get unlimited helpings of fresh pineapple and banana, sweet potato, salt fish cooked with onion, black pepper and tomato, *escoveitch* (sweet-sour fried fish) and johnny cakes." This reflects the happy resurgence of interest in native cookery in the Carribean. Nowadays, after an invigorating rum punch (one part lime juice, two parts sugar, three parts rum and four parts water, ice and a dusting of nutmeg), you eat guava jelly rather than marmalade and put coconut cream in your coffee. There is "pudding and souse" for Sunday brunch—blood sausages, pig's head meat, tongue and trotters, all marinated in lime juice (Trinidad and Barbados). And there are mangoes. The best way to eat one is to cut it in half like an avocado and eat it with a spoon. You might try a chilled orange or avocado soup. On Antigua there are juicy fragrant pawpaws, which you slice like melon, as well as mango jam. *Cassava* bread is fried in butter in Jamaica. The disappearing island Indians—the Caribs—keep a pepper pot on the fire to be dipped into at any time. Tea in the Papiamento dialect—*awa di redu*—delightfully means "gossip water."

When a Lady Nugent, wife of the then governor of Jamaica, paid an official visit to Barbados (long a fierce rival) in 1800, she recorded in her diary that the people "eat like cormorants and drink like porpoises. I observe some of our party ate at breakfast today as though they had never eaten before. A dish of tea, another of coffee, a bumper of claret, another of hoch negus. Then madeira, sangeree [a spiced port wine], hot and cold meats, stews and pies, peppers and gingers, sweetmeats, acid fruits, sweet jellies . . . in short, as astonishing as it was disgusting."

In San Juan, Puerto Rico, there is a sweet breakfast roll baked with lard and dusted with powdered sugar. The island also offers *ostione*, oysters that grow on the underwater roots of the mangrove tree, and ever since the nineteenth century local families have eaten *pan de majorca* with their local coffee. On Jamaica they drink a coffee unique to the island. It is called Blue Mountain and is sometimes flavored with such things as orange rind, cinnamon, allspice, ginger, whipped cream, frozen coconut milk, dark rum.

In Scandinavia the Swedes, Norwegians and Danes breakfast primarily on dairy products, fish and bread. Swedes eat uncooked, cured salmon called *gravlox* seasoned with dill, coarse salt, castor sugar, crushed peppercorns and a sauce of mustard and dill. They have wonderfully fresh ingredients such as eggs which are coded to prove they are not more than forty-eight hours away from the farm. Uncooked, dusty oatmeal is eaten with milk and sugar. At Christmas time each place at breakfast is set with something called a *julhög*—"yule pile"—made up of coarse rye bread, fine wheat bread strewn with sugar and chopped almonds, a saffron bun with raisins, a heart-shaped biscuit, and a big red apple on top.

The Danes are famous for their pastries in which they incorporate custards, almonds and jams. They love to eat cold dishes like radishes, smoked eel, smoked salmon, buttered bread and a wide variety of cheeses—perhaps a Tybo with caraway seeds or a Danish Brie or the marvelous new Crèma Dania. An old rural dish is rice porridge with milk and a "butter hole." Herring is another widespread breakfast favorite. One especially thirst-inducing kind is soaked overnight to reduce its saltiness. *Øllebrød* soup is fashioned from sweet beer and stale rye crusts to which milk is added. Often there is a mid-morning *tidbid* of cheese, meat, bread, beer or *snaps* or *aquavit*, that iced fire of a drink, just to keep going.

Norwegians like big breakfasts—herring and other salted fish, several breads, pastries, cheeses, hot and cold cereals, soft-boiled or fried eggs, bacon, potatoes, fruit and fruit juice, milk, buttermilk, sour milk, coffee and tea. They are very fond of sour cream. Among other dishes the Scandinavians enjoy there is *rårakor*—grated raw potatoes, salt, pepper and chives dropped, a tablespoon at a time, into a hot lightly oiled and buttered frying pan and spread out into a golden lace; sour-cream waffles called *fløtevafler*; cherry tomatoes stuffed with cream cheese and bacon. The Lapps like to salt their coffee. The Danes and Swedes add *aquavit* or vodka to theirs—the former calling the concoction "a little black one" and the latter "coffee cuckoo." A foolproof way to fix it is to place a 10 øre piece (about the size of an American dime) at the bottom of a cup, pour coffee into it until the coin disappears, and then alcohol until it *re*appears. In Finland spinach pancakes and crullers are breakfast favorites. Coffee seems to be drunk all day long accompanied by pastries, coffee cakes, onion rolls, doughnuts, waffles.

The Dutch still enjoy splendid old-fashioned breakfasts made up of soft-boiled eggs, young cheese and pink Ghelderland ham, soft rolls ("cadets"), rye bread (for the ham), raisin bread (for the cheese), breakfast cake (a spiced ginger one), lots of Friesian butter, tea and a nearby tin of Verkade biscuits. In May the Dutch snack on new "green" herring sold from carts. Pieces of the fish are served with minced onion. Or they might stop for a pancake with jam or fruit or syrup to be eaten with steaming chocolate or a coffee.

The Japanese prefer soups for breakfast. Their favorites, known as *miso*, are clear and flavored with soya-bean paste. *Akadashi* is red and garnished with thin slices of white radish (*daikon*) and tiny rings of spring onions. *Shiro Dashi* is white and garnished with tied *kanpyo*, gourd shavings and a dab of hot mustard. There is a glorious clear winter melon soup with prawns garnished with lime rind. *Misoshiru* is a rich soup with a spoon of soya bean added to each serving along with fermented rice paste and garnishes. *Tamago Dashimaki* is a flaky rolled omelette filled with layers of *nori* (a type of seaweed) and egg and served with grated white radish. There are dawn tea ceremonies of great beauty and formality. But tea is drunk round-the-clock. A traditional first item on the menu are *umeboshi*, tiny red pickled plums which are *very* sour. Along with the ubiquitous tea, there is a classic dish consisting of a heaping bowl of rice sprinkled with *nori* or other garnishes, and another in which a raw egg is whipped and poured over the hot rice to cook. Recently pancakes have been gaining in popularity. Tangerines appear in late December and can be bought in such places as the subway. Very late at night, or very early in the morning, depending on how you look at it, food wagons offer grilled fish, potatoes, eggs, giant radishes, fried soya-bean curd and heart-warming *sake*. Open-air stalls and shops sell skewered bits of chicken, chicken liver and spring onions all impaled on a length of bamboo and brushed with *terujaki* sauce along with quail eggs, green peppers and ginkgo nuts.

In pre-World War I Russia four meals a day were eaten. The day started with tea, very strong and

diluted in the cup with boiling water from the samovar—an ornate urn heated by charcoal. Sugar and milk were added. Women drank from cups but men drank from glasses set in metal holders with handles. With the tea, sweet buns, rolls, bread and butter, sometimes cheese, were served. *Bliny*, the wonderful buckwheat pancakes, are made with a yeast flour and take about six hours to prepare. They are served with butter and sour cream or spread with red caviar or some smoked fish. Usually no sour cream is added to black caviar. Catherine the Great, who was German, breakfasted only upon bread and coffee, which seems very modern of her. Today, street sellers offer buns and bagels with tea at all hours. The common breakfast is bread and tea and perhaps an egg.

In Central Asia the day begins often with *kump*—a curd preparation rather like yogurt—or a sharp creamy cheese accompanied by a flat bread called *non*, warm from the oven. A hotel in Estonia offers breakfast pancakes—*pannkook*—as big and round as the plate spread with red whortleberry preserves, coffee and rich cakes. Supposedly Latvians like canned peas for breakfast. In the Ukraine you'll find marvelous bread and cakes, doughnut puffs either plain or filled with rose petals (*pampushky*) and layered coffee cakes (*perekladanets*). Wheat, millet, barley and buckwheat are baked or steamed as *kasha* and eaten with milk in some parts of the vast country. In, say, Bukhara a mid-morning snack might be *shashlyke*—skewered lamb, the hot dog of Central Asia. A delicious dumpling called *varenyky* contains cabbage, meat, mushrooms, fish and potatoes and is served with dollops of sour cream. Cheese and fruit are much enjoyed. If you have a hangover in Armenia a "guaranteed restorative" is a big dish of tripe stewed with garlic, pepper and salt in a broth fortified with beaten egg and lemon juice (see "The Mourning After" for other cures).

In Poland they still eat *bigos*, a stew originally served as breakfast in the forests to aristocrats out for a hunt—left-over game, beef, pork, dried mushrooms, cabbage, onions, tomatoes, sausages and apples.

In Switzerland at a lake-side hotel breakfast might consist of cornmeal porridge, smoked bacon, the incomparable Swiss version of fried potatoes known as *rösti* and "coffee-milk." Or traveling on a superscenic railroad, the passenger might order creamy scrambled eggs, crusty rolls, light-as-air *croissants* with honey and jam, and hot milk with coffee served from silver pots. Other travelers might be breakfasting on open sandwiches, plates of sausages, bottles of beer and wine.

Bulgarians enjoy country breakfasts of *Slivovitsa* for a starter and then a thick vegetable soup with lots of meat, farm bread, hard-boiled eggs, garlic sausages, a bowl of yogurt with finely sliced onions and a dish of cherries. *Banitsa* are flaky cheese rolls often eaten with coffee. Sausages of veal and pork and garlic (*kebabcha*) are a favorite snack. As is a salami-like sausage called *laukanka* accompanied by red wine. On autumn days during the grape harvest Romanians like to eat *mititei*—a charcoal-grilled sausage of minced beef and chopped garlic. At six in the morning Romanians in the country have been known to down a glass of plum liqueur (*Tsuica*) and follow it with roast duck and tomatoes, yellow maize soup, brown bread, fresh sheep's cheese, hard-boiled eggs, hot milk and an apple. The preference among country and city folk in Eastern Europe and the Balkans for an alcoholic eye-opener is continued in Hungary with their famed raspberry liqueur known as *Tokaj*. A traditional farmhouse breakfast might include fragrant brown wheat bread, a thick slice of streaky bacon covered in paprika powder, yellow peppers or some other vegetable just picked from the garden, a glass of hot milk and a bunch of grapes.

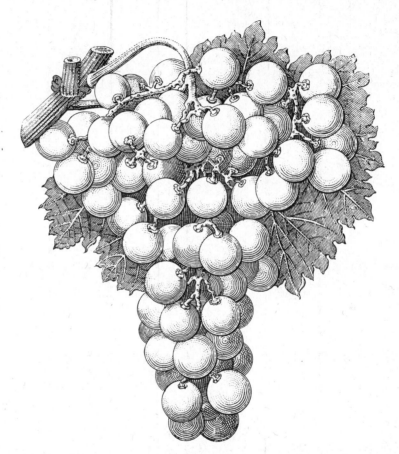

The Mourning After

Like practically everything on this earth having to do with human beings there are as many experts and as many theories about hangover treatment as there are people. And no matter how ingeniously one goes about postponing the question of eating, eventually that first meal will have to be faced. Those of us who have had to cope with the problem with fair regularity over the years have discovered through desperate trial and hideous error the sometimes weird chemistry of our own best cure.

Many subscribe to the classic Alka-Seltzer and long lie-down. There are the Coca-Cola adherents; the thick malted or milk shake adherents (the idea being to "line the stomach"); the steak tartar buffs. There are believers in eggs—cooked or raw; mushrooms or tomatoes on toast; grilled chicken livers; Vichyssoise or Borscht; cheese served in various ways. There are lots of gallons-of-black-coffee freaks; nothing-but-milk believers. Fernet-Branca. Cold beer. Steam baths. Oxygen inhaling. . . . Typically, with the latter two we've come full circle to the avoidance of the main issue—i.e., food.

A general theory is that vitamin B is very important as a death-deterrent. I've known maddeningly overorganized people who have the habit of downing doses of vitamins *before* going to bed the night before. Lots of people swear by aspirin. None of these constitute anything that could be called a breakfast.

In the January 1976 issue of the British *Vogue*, Henry McNulty suggested several ideas for an "imbiber's breakfast": plain yogurt with honey or cooked with leaf spinach (press out the water) and topped with sour cream and a few minced mint leaves. You can even add a fried egg (I personally find all fried foods impossible in such circumstances). Mr. McNulty also offers a baked egg: fry sausage patties and place in an oven-proof dish, break two eggs over the sausage and season with salt and pepper. Add a tablespoon of tomato sauce and top with bread crumbs mixed with softened butter. Bake at 350° F. for 15 minutes.

Mr. McNulty shares my views about the reviving quality of soups. He offers two: *Mongole*—one tin/can each of tomato and pea soups, cream, an equal amount of water, one teaspoon of sugar, two teaspoons Worcestershire sauce, salt, pepper, three tablespoons Valdespino sherry, sour cream. To the soups and water add the cream and other ingredients, except for the sherry and sour cream. Cook slowly until the soup is smooth and remove from heat. Blend in the sherry and sour cream. *Cold yogurt soup* begins with thin slices of cucumber (about one medium one per person—which suggests, very odd thought, that you're in a mood for entertaining!) placed in a bowl and seasoned with salt and pepper. Rub a separate bowl with a clove of garlic and then chop up the clove. Swish a teaspoon of vinegar around with the garlic. Add a small container of plain yogurt and a teaspoon of dill. Stir till smooth. Pour over cucumbers. Sprinkle with olive oil and lemon juice.

Of course you may have a cold soup recipe of your own. The idea, psychologically if not physiologically, is to please and revive the mind as well as the stomach, to seduce you back among the living. A wonderful and very attractive soup is the great Spanish classic Gazpacho (in Spain the details differ from province to province). I like it served the way I first experienced it in a tile-cool restaurant in Barcelona—with little side dishes of chopped tomatoes, cucumbers, green peppers, onions, and croutons made with butter and garlic. The soup itself is made of the same tomatoes, cucumbers, peppers, onions and garlic blended in an electric blender, strained into a bowl and chilled. The redoubtable Robert Carrier in *The Cookery of Spain and Portugal* suggests stirring in a mixture of blended olive oil, lemon juice, salt, tomato juice and cayenne pepper.

Vichyssoise consists of potatoes, peeled and cut into small pieces, cooked in salted water; leeks, split and sautéed in butter; chicken broth added to leeks. When tender, put both the potatoes and the leeks through a sieve, combine with chicken broth. Blend. Chill for twenty-four hours. Serve in chilled bowls adding heavy or sour cream and a few finely chopped chives. Most general cookbooks contain recipes for these soups along with little variations.

Perhaps one last classic is called for. It may seem odd in the gray miserable light of a hung-over morn, but if you imagine that you are in Les Halles in Paris at 5 A.M. surrounded by porters and workmen instead of alone in the silence of your lonely room. . . . All right, I *am* asking too much and we all know that Les Halles is no longer there. But if you really *like* onion soup then my belief in the pleasure principle as an important part of your cure will work. *Soupe a l'oignon* is a glorious combination of peeled and sliced onions sautéed *very* slowly in butter until brown, with beef stock added bit by bit. The whole stirred until boiling. Lower heat and simmer for an hour or so. Carrier adds about an ounce (per serving) of cognac, salt and pepper just before serving and accompanies the dish with toasted buttered French bread generously heaped with grated Gruyère. James Beard in *The James Beard Cookbook* suggests adding a little Kitchen Bouquet for those who enjoy a deep brown soup. This is done during the first stage while the onions are being sautéed. After the soup comes to a boil, he adds sherry, seasoning to taste, and grated Emmental or Gruyère cheese. The mixture is then poured into a casserole and baked at 350° F. for 15 minutes. Serve topped with toasted buttered bread sprinkled with Parmesan cheese—a nice duet of two cheeses. Carrier's "oven version" directs you to fill oven-proof dishes with oven-toasted bread "covering each layer with freshly grated Gruyère," filling each bowl with onion soup and baking in preheated oven (450° F.) until cheese is "bubbling and golden brown."

The great advantage of most soups is that they may already exist in one form or another in the refrigerator and you won't have to expose your delicate condition to the hazards of cooking. But depending on the strength and character of your hangover there are breakfast dishes described in other parts of this book you might want to try. Remember it's your head and your stomach.

I have left until now the liquid approach—i.e., alcoholic. The world has long known of something brutally labeled "the-hair-of-the-dog-that-bit-you." Again we have innumerable formulas and variations. We also have our classics, our perennial tops-of-the-props. The simplest and greatest is as good a champagne as you can afford. If the one you can afford isn't all that extraordinary mix it with an equal amount of fresh orange juice.

Before leaving champagne entirely behind I'd like to offer the Champagne Cocktail. In a chilled 14–16 ounce stemmed glass (so your hand won't warm the drink) pour 3 to 4 ounces fine chilled cognac. This over a lump of sugar doused with Angostura bitters. Fill with champagne and add a spiral of lime.

An effort to raise the dead: Alice Brady being served by a penguin-like William Powell, the millionaire masquerading as a butler, in My Man Godfrey *(1936).*

Less royal perhaps but widely advocated are such things as the Bloody Mary, Screw Driver, Prairie Oyster, Bull Shot. I'm rather taken with the lucid prescription attributed to the great jazz man Eddie Conden: "Take the juice of one quart of Scotch . . ."

The Prairie Oyster has been immortalized in a way in John Van Druten's play *I Am a Camera* after Christopher Isherwood's story about Sally Bowles. When Sally first meets Chris she exclaims that she's "allergic to coffee. I come out in the most sinister spots if I drink it before dinner . . . I always have Prairie Oysters for breakfast. Don't you adore them? Eggs with Worcester Sauce all sort of wooshed up together. I simply live on them." Three months later she offers one to a German friend, Fritz, who has never had the pleasure. Sally mixes them with a pen (sometimes she uses a thermometer!) and Fritz proceeds to choke on his. When asked what's the matter, he replies that "It is a little painful" and asks if they should be drunk down all at once. Sally answers that they are better that way, "Especially when you are not feeling well. They sort of come back at you."

Charles H. Baker, Jr., in his unique *The Gentleman's Companion* (1939) has this to say: "We once had a shipmate who insisted on a morning dip in Long Island Sound even in November; just as we have other hardy friends who eat enormous cream oyster stews for mornings after, or toss off Prairie Oysters, which seen eye to eye would simply mean one gyration of our adam's apple and a free ticket to a marble slab in the morgue. . . ." He lists these ingredients:

Egg yolk, in its unbroken state
Salt, good pinch
Lemon juice, 1 tsp
Worcestershire, 1 tsp
Ketchup, 1 tsp
Vinegar, ½ tsp
Tabasco, 1 drop
Cayenne, pinch on top

His drinking instructions: "Shut eyes, open mouth, murmur prayers for the soul, pop in and swallow whole. . . . This *has* been administered for the evening before, but its benefits have proven to be base canard, a sorry snare and delusion."

Of the many Bloody Marys I've experienced, my favorite is served in the bar of the delightful Swiss Hotel in Sonoma, California. It was concocted by owner Ted Dunlap and its "secret" is the lemon pepper. Over a tall glass with ice in it pour 1 ounce vodka. Add 2 shakes lemon pepper, 2 shakes celery salt, 1 drop Tabasco, ½ teaspoon Worcestershire sauce, squeeze of lime. Fill glass with tomato juice and stir—preferably with a stalk of crisp celery. Variations abound. Add a raw egg. Use the distinctive V-8 juice. A leading vodka producer even offers an "improvement" on the Bloody Mary: 1½ ounces vodka on ice, fill with tomato juice, add horseradish to taste. Name? "Horseshot" (somewhat dangerous in areas of verbal imprecision I would think). According to Jill Newman writing in *Gentlemen's Quarterly* (March 1976), the Bloody Mary is the "fourth most popular drink of the seventies" (in the U.S. one assumes) following the martini (this means "dry martini," a mixture of gin or vodka with vermouth), Manhattan and whiskey sour. In its favor for many is its near smell-less and tasteless vodka (not true of the best Russian or Polish however) and its protein and vitamin-rich (lots of A and C), only-3-calories-per-ounce tomato juice. *GQ* lists several interesting variations: the Legal Seafood Restaurant in Cambridge, Massachusetts, uses shrimp as a garnish and mixes a tequila version called Red Mist; New York's Trader Vic's substitutes light Puerto Rican rum; the Hotel Pontchartrain in New Orleans adds a quarter ounce of beef bouillon; the Delegates' Lounge of the United Nations adds onion juice and grated horseradish; the cartoonist Charles Adams uses one part clam juice to one part tomato juice, a slug of vodka, dash of Tabasco. It's a wide-open field for experimentation. Question: If made with gin could one call it "Bloody Ginger" after the fiery dancer?

The great Screw Driver is almost embarrassingly simple: $1\frac{1}{2}$ ounces of vodka, 3 to 4 ounces of orange juice (fresh please!) over ice. That's all there is to it.

Curiously, not widely known but surely a classic and a superb counter to the pounding head, is the Sazarac Cocktail, an extraordinary drink associated with New Orleans. Like most great drinks it is extremely simple. Baker agrees with me that the glass is important—"big thick-bottomed," about twice the size of an Old Fashioned glass. "Reason: thick walls keep the strong mixed liquor cold; and *warm* strong mixed liquor is like a chemical in the nostrils and throat. . . ." Liquor and glass *must* be pre-chilled. Coat interior of glass with several squirts of absinthe or Pernod (120 proof) and spin glass between your hands to be sure liquid is spread evenly; pour 2 ounces rye whiskey (the best you can afford) into a shaker, add 3 or 4 squirts of Peychard's bitters. Shake hard with big pieces of ice. Strain into your prepared glass and twist a long thin peel of lemon on top. Smell as you would brandy. *Sip.*

The Daiquiri is another classic especially effective the morning after. According to Baker (and one is inclined to believe him for his *style* if nothing else) this drink was invented in the summer of 1898 in Daiquiri, a village near Santiago and the Bacardi plant in Cuba. This original drink consisted of $1\frac{1}{2}$ ounces Bacardi rum, 2 teaspoons sugar, the juice (strained) of $1\frac{1}{2}$ small green limes, and finely cracked ice. These were shaken and transferred to a tall cocktail glass. Nowadays, they can all be put into a blender. Baker suggests only *one* teaspoon of sugar and a Manhattan glass as more substantial.

Try also his Ramos Fizz or Original Gin Fizz. Again, associated with New Orleans. First the shaker is iced with a tumbler of cracked ice. Then the ingredients—1 jigger Old Tom gin (which has an oily texture and a slight orange taste), 1 teaspoon sugar, 3 or 4 drops orange flower water, white of 1 egg, 2 tablespoons cream, juice (strained) of $\frac{1}{2}$ lime and $\frac{1}{2}$ lemon. Shake for at least a minute and strain into chilled thin goblet. Add as much chilled club soda as you like. A blender can be used, but use only about a quarter goblet of ice.

My last "reliance" on Mr. Baker and his *Gentleman's Companion*, to cheer us all up, ends with a variation on the champagne cocktail. He "stumbled" into it in the French Concession of Shanghai in those long ago days before World War II and supposedly the formula came out of White Russia. It is called the Imperial Cossack Crusta and is made as follows: "Take a large champagne glass, and ice it well. Split a green lime, or lemon, lengthwise and rub its combined oils and juices over the whole inside of the crystal, and then on out and down a full $\frac{1}{2}''$ below the rim. First dip this lip into powdered sugar, then fill the whole glass with sugar—emptying it out and permitting what sticks to remain. . . . Now add 2 dashes of orange bitters, 1 jigger of cognac and $\frac{1}{2}$ that of kümmel, stirring for a moment in a bar glass with 3 ice cubes. Empty this into the goblet, fill with chilled dry champagne, toss in a scarlet rose petal and think of slender, pliable Russian princesses and things!"

If none of these inspiriting beverages turn out to suit your system there are always the aptly named Bitters (self-punishment by way of atonement?). There's famed Fernet-Branca, an Italian concoction from Milan mysteriously composed of some witches brew of "exotic" (the label only states "*esotici*") ingredients and with a compelling proof of 70 degrees, the taste of which has been described by Humphrey Lyttelton as an "elusive blend of syrup of figs and mothballs." This can be modified by the addition of an equal part of Italian sweet vermouth, 2 parts gin, shaken with ice.

There's also the equally famed Underberg, German this time. Even more "proofy"—84 degrees. The fact that it looks like and tastes like cough syrup adds to the effectiveness of penance-doing. For the best results it should be downed in one gulp like a shot of whiskey. It too disdains to tell us what it is made of. Not true of herbal bitters like Galixir. The taste is quite as horrific but the "makings" are given as—among other things—wormwood, dandelion, and St. Mary's thistle. Or you can resort to a straight herbal tea like marjoram brewed from the dried or fresh versions.

But there is such a thing as too much atonement and too much self-punishment. I feel that the sheer deliciousness of the soups and drinks I've described can make of hideous headache and baleful gaze a way toward unexpected delights—so much so that they seem more than worth the having to live through.

American Ways

"... the first food I remember from my early childhood in San Francisco in the early eighties is breakfast food: cracked wheat with sugar and cream, corn meal with molasses, and farina with honey."

Alice B. Toklas

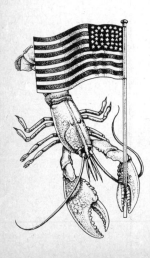

Americans, in spite of the hard and good work of numberless nutritionists, seem to be continuing their drive from appetite to apathy as noted way back in 1954 by *Sports Illustrated* (September 6). At that time two surveys indicated a steady decline in breakfast habits. A five-year study of New Jersey industrial workers carried out by a team from Rutgers University showed that two out of five men polled ate little, if any, breakfast. Four percent ate no breakfast; eleven percent only drank coffee; twenty-six percent breakfasted on sweet rolls or toast and coffee. The other poll—of 10,000 junior and senior high school students in California—revealed that as many as thirty-two percent never or only sometimes ate any breakfast.

As far as I know this hasn't changed much. Or, perhaps, *is* changing in subtle ways. Because of better and better cook books, or the exposure on television of people demonstrating intelligent cookery—Julia Child and James Beard to name only two—or the increased worldliness of Americans traveling all over the place, whatever, I sense a shift toward better and more varied morning meals. At least with people who pay attention to the serious writers on diet and delight in eating.

One of the outstanding developments is a new consciousness about local, regional foods and the real pleasure one can get from them. One of the truly superb books in the valuable Time-Life "Foods of the World" series is *American Cooking* by Dale Brown. He tells of travelers to the United States who experienced their first Plantation Breakfast—"... great bowls of grits [hominy finely ground and cooked in water] ... cream chipped beef, spiced apples, fried bacon, pork sausages; eggs 'sunny-side up' and 'once-over-lightly.' " Large Virginia hams, fried chicken, toast and breads, buckwheat pancakes. He writes of pecan waffles with honey eaten in Charleston, South Carolina, or a "summer breakfast" of grits, boiled shrimps, chilled garden-ripe tomatoes. He describes the Creole cooking of New Orleans in Louisiana—a marvelous mix of French, Spanish, Anglo-Saxon, Indian and Negro cooking involving crabs, oysters, crawfish, hot pepper sauce, filé powder (finely crushed sassafras leaves), thyme, bay leaf and garlic. The seafood fresh from the Gulf of Mexico.

Having mentioned New Orleans, it is impossible not to speak about Brennan's, arguably the most famous purveyors of breakfast in the world. It was begun by an inspired Irishman in 1945 who noticed

Breakfast
at Brennan's®

a tradition that is truly unforgettable

Turn back the clock to the time when the French aristocrats of New Orleans dined in leisurely elegance, when breakfast was served in the patio amidst the soft rustle of exotic plants, a refreshing breeze from palmetto fans and the romantic aroma of magnolia blossoms. Every dish was a delight and the proper wine complemented each course. You can become part of this tradition, recaptured at Brennan's. Start off with an "eye opener" that will awaken you and your appetite. An unhurried breakfast with a wine of your choice should follow. And, for the finale, have one of Brennan's famous desserts and café au lait. Take your time, because this will be the most unforgettable breakfast you'll ever have.

A New Orleans way to start the day: breakfast at Brennan's.

that most restaurants in town didn't open until lunch or dinner and felt that a lot of local people, not to mention tourists, might enjoy something other than the commonplace for breakfast. He even chose the morning cock—symbol of wakefulness—as his logo. Brennan's is a truly French Creole establishment with the kind of drama and color that implies. Located on Royal Street in the Vieux Carré, or French Quarter, it occupies an eighteenth-century house once owned by Degas's grandfather.

The menu is indeed extraordinary. Here are a few of its dishes: for "eye-openers," Milk Punch or Absinthe Suissesse or a Sazerac (see "The Mourning After"). Then perhaps Oyster Soup or a Hot Spiced Baked Apple with Double Cream or Creole Turtle Soup. Then Chicken Livers Sautéed in Red Wine with Mushrooms, Eggs St. Charles (poached eggs on crisply fried trout with Hollandaise sauce), or Roasted Quail in a Potato Nest with a Burgundy Sauce and Diced Artichoke Hearts over Wild Rice. Bananas Foster, Sautéed in Butter, Brown Sugar and Spices and Flamed in Rum and Banana Liqueur and Served over Vanilla Ice Cream. Something called "A Traditional Brennan's Breakfast" as prepared in antebellum days reads: Oyster Soup, Eggs Benedict, Sirloin Steak with Mushrooms, French Bread, Bananas Foster and hot Chicory Coffee. Another of their famed specialties is "Café-Brûlot," so-called after the brûlot bowl which is set over an alcohol flame and involves cinnamon, cloves, orange and lemon peel, and sugar lumps all mashed together. Then brandy and curaçao are added, the brandy ignited, and the whole thing stirred until the sugar has dissolved. Black coffee is then added gradually and the mixing continues until the flame dies out.

Until just recently a visitor to New Orleans could choose between the Morning Call or the Café du Monde in the early hours of the day for superb coffee and doughnuts. But the Morning Call has moved some nine miles out into the suburbs leaving only the Café du Monde at which to taste the *beignets*—sugar-coated, *holeless* doughnuts—and the distinctive chicoried coffee of the area.

Harriet Martineau, an English woman traveling all over the country in the early 1800s, tasted her first hominy in Sweet Springs, Tennessee, and breakfasted in Massachusetts on "excellent bread, potatoes, hung beef, eggs and strong tea." She experienced her first fish chowder at Gloucester. She ate cornbread and buckwheat cakes in Montgomery, Alabama. Another English traveler, a man this time, wrote of Virginia in the *London Magazine* for July 1746 that he'd breakfasted on hashed and fricasseed meats, venison pie, coffee, tea, chocolate, punch, beer and cider. In the 1880s Alessandro Filippini, the chef of the fashionable New York restaurant Delmonico's, published "The Table" containing three menus for every day in the year. For a Sunday in July he suggested an omelette with asparagus tips, grilled kingfish, chicken hash *à la crème*, sweet potatoes, Hollandaise sauce and a Milan cake.

In the Southwest and Far West the cowboys were served by their "doughbelly" from the chuck wagon that went with them and the cattle. Their diet featured beans—usually Pinto beans—bacon, salt pork. Some called their beans by the delightful moniker "Mexican strawberries." They ate pan-fried potatoes; dried fruits; canned goods, like tomatoes, when they could get them; flapjacks, so-called because the pancakes are flipped over; vinegar pie—beaten eggs and sugar flavored with boiled vinegar; "Nigger in a Blanket"—thick dough folded around raisins soaked in brandy; biscuits; "Texas butter"—lard in which steak had cooked, extended with water and flour to make a gravy; sorghum and syrup from dried fruits; wild berries in season—blackberries, raspberries, huckleberries and salmon berries. Sourdough bread is still famous in the West. (Tourists in San Francisco love to buy contemporary versions of it to carry home.) The cook took salt and flour, water and a bit of sugar and put them out in the sun to ferment and collect wild yeasts from the air. He carried this dough with him as a precious possession, replacing water and flour as he used it. Some have been known to remain active for fifty years! The cook would take a discarded lard can or a large pan, put in a large quantity of flour, some salt, a little sugar and add sourdough in the center until he had the dough he wanted. Then he would knead it, let it rise, form it into loaves, let it rise a second time, put it into his Dutch oven, cover, place the oven in hot coals, put more hot coals on the galleried top, and bake. (Along with a skillet and a coffee pot a Dutch oven was essential to the cowboy cook. It is a round iron vessel with a cover and sometimes legs.) Biscuits were made by adding soda or baking powder to the flour. By taking this biscuit mixture, or some of the sourdough, a pudding, a little like a suet, was made with raisins and fruit added. This was called "Son-of-a-Bitch-in-a-Sack" because it was put in a sack to boil for a long period.

Meat was always a problem—feast or famine, lots of butchering but no refrigeration. Boiled testicles were very popular. Steaks and pot roasts and stews were the norm. One stew was the most popular of all. It was called "Son-of-a-Bitch Stew" and consisted of what we would call offal: the heart, liver, marrow gut, tenderloin, sweetbreads and brains of a freshly killed animal, preferably a calf, cooked in a pot—small pieces of heart first as it was the toughest, then the rest after soaking in water, a handful at a time. Last of all, the brains. Then some flour, the blood, salt, pepper, sometimes an onion (amusingly dubbed "skunk egg"). Great care had to be taken not to scorch the stew. Chili powder was sometimes added as well. The marrow gut was considered essential to a good stew. This is a tube connecting two of the stomach's four sections in a cud-chewing animal. In a calf it is filled with a substance that helps

the animal to digest the mother cow's milk. A cowboy saying goes: "A son-of-a-bitch might not have any brains and no heart, but if he don't have guts, he's no son-of-a-bitch."

Today, big-city breakfasts, as typified by a town like New York, vary in cultural and ethnic ways, but are fairly universal otherwise. They are made up of the usual litany of coffee or tea, of eggs one way of another, of breads and jams, of bacon or steak. But for many, the real enchantment comes when such ethnic favorites as *panetone* or herring or bagels are added.

The city breakfast ranges from a cup of instant coffee drunk while dressing to go to work, to the joys of some delicatessen celebrated for its lox, to lazy Sunday brunches at a Fifth Avenue hotel. There are hearty meals of eggs and steak and pancakes eaten at diners across from the docks along the Hudson where the few remaining liners tie up, newly arrived from distant ports. There are countless English muffins buttered by countless harried commuters in countless coffee shops. There are picnic breakfasts in the summer. Hurry-up breakfasts before running off to school. Breakfasts in the early darkness of winter mornings. There are even those who require another kind of food and feast from shop windows, as Truman Capote immortalized in his image of a *Breakfast at Tiffany's*.

Some years ago, crossing from New York to Los Angeles by car and in something of a hurry, it seemed there was no place to eat along the great highways except Howard Johnson's. If I stuck to things like hamburgers, bacon, lettuce and tomato sandwiches, ice cream, or breakfasts, the food was quite good. I found myself, in fact, eating variations of breakfast most of the time. Their menu hasn't changed significantly since then and is typical of American breakfast food: Tomato, grapefruit or orange juice; grapefruit sections or half "in season" (?); stewed prunes; choice of cold cereals with milk—banana optional; hot oatmeal; eggs—scrambled in butter or "any style"; bacon; smoked ham; hashed brown potatoes; French toast with whipped butter and warm syrup; hot cakes with link sausages; blueberry hot cakes; corn bread, English muffins, blueberry squares, Danish pastries; coffee, tea or milk—chocolate for the kids.

Millions of Americans love it.

Cowboy's chow—seated on haunches, hands for a table—beans or Son-of-a-Bitch Stew served up on a tin plate. A scene from Will Perry *(1967), with Charlton Heston looking into the worrying distance.*

Log Cabin Syrup

The syrup I loved as a child, and remember now, is Log Cabin. The reason is simple—it tasted delicious and came in a container roughly shaped like a log cabin with the screw-top opening off-center representing a chimney. Alas, that container is no more. It first disappeared during World War II (all tin plate was taken by the war effort), made a valiant return after the war ended, but disappeared again in 1957 when scarcity of tin and consequent high cost banished it forever. Now it comes in glass—newly designed bottles celebrating the Bicentennial. There are five glass flasks, three of them replicas of early American flasks from the 1850s.

Log Cabin syrup was produced in the 1880s by P. J. Towle, a St. Paul grocer who was dissatisfied with the way corn syrup and molasses were handled and worked out a blend of his own. Nowadays it is a mixture of maple sugar, sugar syrup, corn syrup, flavorings, colorings, and preservatives. To get maple syrup the sap from the trees (referred to as "bushes" by the industry) is sugared off during March and April. The sap begins to

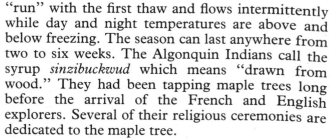

"run" with the first thaw and flows intermittently while day and night temperatures are above and below freezing. The season can last anywhere from two to six weeks. The Algonquin Indians call the syrup *sinzibuckwud* which means "drawn from wood." They had been tapping maple trees long before the arrival of the French and English explorers. Several of their religious ceremonies are dedicated to the maple tree.

Maple bushes are found only on the North American continent and hard maples supply 90 to 95 percent of all syrup produced (although some commercially adaptable sap comes from the soft or red maple). It takes about forty years for a tree to be big enough for commercial tapping. The trees thrive on rich hilly or mountainous soil. They store starch and sugar during the summer. In the winter the starch is converted into sugar. Some of this sugar appears in the spring flow of sap, which is gathered from holes bored in the trees and collected in buckets. The sap is then sent to the sugarhouses to be boiled. It takes about thirty-five gallons of sap to make one gallon of maple syrup. Color and density are important in determining the grade. The highest quality is a light amber and has the most delicate flavor. Medium amber color has a stronger taste. Today, 97 percent of the maple product is syrup, with only 3 percent represented by maple sugar. If you search it out, it is possible to find pure maple syrup on the market.

Hunt Breakfast

Maine, Autumn of '54

Three hours before sunrise, the low moan of the cow moose was heard in the land—well, in Old Town's city park. It was calling together 1,600 Maine deer hunters to the opening of the deer season. The caller was Chief Bruce Poolan of the Penobscot Indians.

Men from twenty-seven states responded, lining up for what was described by *Sports Illustrated* (November 1, 1954) as "a lumberjack's menu of 4,300 biscuits, 400 pounds of ham, 87 gallons of coffee, and 3,700 doughnuts. No one counted the beans which had been baking . . . in the ground all night . . ."

The breakfast in the chill morning, around hardwood fires, ceremonially announced that, after sunrise, it was legal to hunt deer in Aroostook, Somerset, Piscataquis, Franklin and Penobscot counties. After the slightly later opening of the season throughout the rest of the state, about 175,000 hunters were expected to go after their venison.

Old Town was just about deserted, and the food had run out by eight o'clock. The hunters had headed into the big woods for about fifty miles around. "At noon, a Washington, D.C., physician bagged his first deer—a magnificent 15-point buck that field-dressed at 217 pounds. Good hunting everyone said."

On the Screen

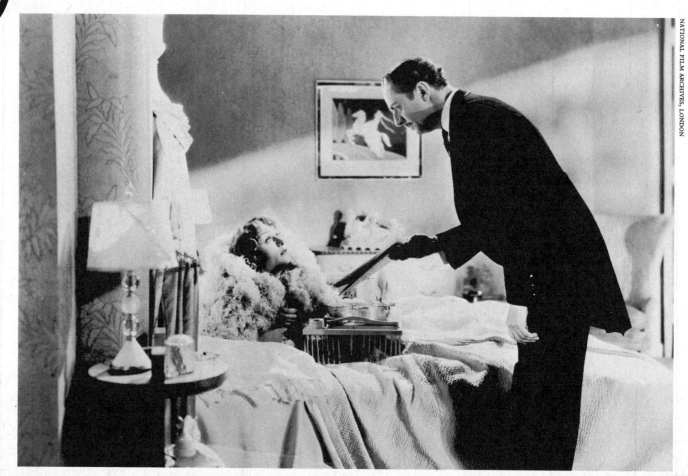

An unforgettable butler—William Powell in My Man Godfrey *(1936). But of course he's not really a butler at all. He's a millionaire in disguise out to teach a spoiled family several lessons. The wonderfully funny Carol Lombard is the person having breakfast in bed. Alice Brady, the mother of the household, has already received her breakfast in "The Mourning After"* *(see p. 68).*

"Maybe you've found someone you like better?" Probably the most famous half-grapefruit in the world. The scene shocked the public and sent James Cagney's career soaring to new heights—or, more appropriately, depths. "A gentleman doesn't hit a lady." But, of course, this was no gentleman and she's no lady. The tough, "realistic" gangster and his victim (Mae Clark). The film is The Public Enemy *(1931).*

Sheer wit. The enchanting comedy It Happened One Night *(1934)—an up-dating of* The Taming of the Shrew—*with the new twist of a wealthy, spoiled girl in the midst of the Depression pursued by a new hero : the cynical newspaper reporter with a heart of gold. In this scene Clark Gable teaches Claudette Colbert the proper way to dunk doughnuts.*

One of the most imaginative uses of breakfast in the history of the cinema is the three-minute sequence of breakfasts in Orson Welles and Herman J. Mankiewicz's Citizen Kane (1940). The sequence shows the deterioration of Kane's first marriage from the years 1901 to 1909 and are handled as flashbacks recounted by Kane's old friend Jed Leland (Joseph Cotton in the film). The two stills show Kane and Emily in one of the final stages of their marriage.

Dogma

"The general rule, however, is to eat breakfast like a king, lunch like a prince, and dinner like a pauper."

Adelle Davis

When it comes to the business of what to eat, how much to eat and when to eat, there arises the considerable dilemma of whom to believe. Well, like religion, you choose your church. There are many faiths. Adelle Davis, Richard Mackarness, and Gaylord Hauser are three I find quite convincing.

"You determine how you will feel throughout each day by the type of breakfast you eat. You can produce inefficiency in yourself by eating too little food or too much of the wrong kind of food." Thus Adelle Davis in her chapter on breakfast in her book *Let's Eat Right to Keep Fit*. It is a very readable and clearly argued work. Ms. Davis goes on to speak of the amount and *quality* of sugar in the blood that breakfast establishes and the energy produced by the burning of this sugar, either alone or combined with fat. Something called "fasting blood sugar" is the amount of sugar found in the blood after a period of twelve hours without food. It averages 90 to 95 mg per 100 cc of blood. When this figure falls to around 70 mg, fatigue and hunger begin to set in. A rumbling stomach or mad desire for something sweet begins when the blood sugar drops to around

65 mg. Lower than that and things become really unpleasant with headaches and heart palpitations, even vomiting. Blackouts and fainting can even occur because the brain derives its energy *only* from sugar.

According to some of the many studies being made of blood sugar levels, to drink black coffee alone is a foolish exercise. The morning grows worse and worse as the blood sugar count drops. Sugar in coffee plus a sweet roll or doughnut will cause the blood sugar to rise rapidly, *but* an hour later it will drop again and you are back at the fatigue, inefficiency point. A typical American breakfast was tested—orange juice, two pieces of bacon, toast and jam, coffee with cream and sugar. The blood sugar rapidly rose, but it *fell* within an hour far below the pre-breakfast level and remained below normal until lunchtime. Next, the same foods were eaten and oatmeal with sugar and milk was added. This time the blood sugar rose rapidly only to fall quickly to a *lower* level than in any of the other tests. By adding to the same "typical" breakfast eight ounces of whole milk with $2\frac{1}{2}$ tablespoons of powdered skim milk, the blood sugar rose and *stayed* at about 120 mg for the rest of the morning.

Next, two eggs replaced the fortified milk. Again "a high level of efficiency was maintained" throughout the morning. The last test was the "typical" breakfast with both eggs and fortified milk added and larger amounts of toast and jam. Result:

efficiency was maintained once again. Furthermore, testing people's well-being in the afternoon showed that those who had eaten eggs and/or fortified milk had a high blood sugar count all afternoon. Those whose blood sugar had been low in the morning experienced a lift after lunch but only for a very short time, whereupon their blood sugar level fell for the rest of the afternoon.

Other tests showed that a high-carbohydrate breakfast—the "typical" breakfast plus a packaged cereal—produced the quick rise, followed by a fall to a low-levels pattern. A high-fat breakfast—a packaged cereal with whipped cream—produced only a slight rise but it held for the rest of the morning. A high-protein meal—lean beef, cottage cheese, skim milk—produced outstanding results: blood sugar rose slowly to 120 mg and remained at that level for the following six hours. Metabolism also rose and remained high for the same six hours.

The best results depend on protein along with *some* fat and *some* carbohydrate according to Ms. Davis. Only when sugar is combined with protein and fat is it absorbed into the blood at a gradual rate maintaining a high level for many hours. In the "typical" breakfast described, the intake of lots of sugar produces a sudden dramatic rise in blood sugar which, with the aid of insulin, is broken down into starch, glycogen or fat, which the body then stores. But as digestion continues, sugar keeps entering the blood. This ultimately defeats the purpose for which the sugar was initially taken—to create energy. The more carbohydrates eaten, the more insulin is oversupplied and the more sugar is *withdrawn* ending in fatigue.

If three high-carbohydrate meals are eaten a day the insulin overproduction can become really serious and even lead to insulin shock. Cells cannot store very much glycogen so that the rest of the sugar intake changes into fat. As the stored glycogen/sugar is depleted the sugar necessary to convert fat into energy is missing and the brain and nerves turn to the adrenals which "send out cortisone, and cells are destroyed so that their protein can be converted in part to sugar." It is a vicious circle of over- and undersupply.

If, however, breakfast supplies "a small amount of sugar and fat along with moderate protein, digestion takes place slowly; sugar trickles into the blood, giving a sustained pickup hour after hour. Insulin production is not overstimulated. Glycogen storage proceeds normally; no hated fat is formed. Energy urges the body into activity; warmth is produced as needed, or the cooling system functions with equal efficiency if the weather is hot."

The studies also showed that only when 22 grams or more of protein were produced did efficiency last for three hours after the meal. The six-hour efficiency mentioned was the result of 55 grams of protein being produced. In order to maintain high-level blood sugar, eating between meals was tried.

The objection to this is the danger of gaining weight. Of such means studied so far, a glass of whole milk along with 100 calories of fresh fruit produced the greatest efficiency.

Typical American eating habits result in the efficiency production occurring *after* the evening meal only to be slept away! Ms. Davis suggests that the best way to launch a campaign of efficiency is to eat a "mid-meal" in the late afternoon. Then have a *simple* dinner avoiding potatoes, gravy, desserts. Because you have not overeaten and haven't eaten the wrong things, you will be hungry for breakfast the next morning and "when hungry, one always finds time to eat."

Dr. Richard Mackarness, in *Eat Fat and Grow Slim* (1975), repeats the findings of William Banting as told in his book *Letter on Corpulence* published by himself in 1864. Mr. Banting weighed 202 pounds and was 5 feet 5 inches tall. Following a diet given to him by a man named William Harvey (*not* the discoverer of the circulation of the blood), he weighed 156 pounds a year later. For breakfast he was allowed four or five ounces of beef, mutton, kidneys, bacon or cold meat of any kind; broiled fish; one small biscuit or one ounce of dry toast; and a large cup of tea without milk or sugar. Dr. Mackarness comments: "Incidentally, I know of no particular reason why salmon and pork should be excluded." Banting concluded from his experience,

"I can now confidently say that *quantities* of diet may be safely left to the natural appetite, and that it is the *quality* only which is essential to abate and cure corpulence."

Lots of doctors refused to go along with this diet and altered it to read *lean* meat thereby restricting fat as well as carbohydrate. Whereas Banting's diet was a "high-fat, high-protein, unrestricted calorie diet with only carbohydrate restricted." Banting was also allowed 24 ounces of meat, poultry or fish per day along with alcohol and other things amounting to 2,800 calories daily.

Mackarness has this to say about overeating: "Two people of the same size, doing the same work, and eating the same food will react differently when they overeat."

"The first thing to realize is that it is carbohydrate (starch and sugar) and *carbohydrate only* which fattens fat people."

"Why does a [person] fail to burn up the excess [fat]? *Because he has a defective capacity for dealing with carbohydrates.*"

Butter: "We now know that it may be freely eaten without causing weight gain."

Meat: "Meat with fat is *not* fattening however much you eat, so long as you eat it without any carbohydrate."

Quantity: The amount eaten is left to natural appetite—eat fat and protein in palatable proportions of "one part fat to three parts lean. . . ."

In a list titled "Stop! *Never eat these*!!" Dr. Mackarness lists these foods related to breakfast: biscuits, bread, cornflour, breakfast cereals, crisp breads, flour, macaroni and other pastas, buns of all kinds, dried fruits such as prunes and figs, canned fruits in heavy syrup, sugar, chocolate confectionary of all kinds, jams, honey and marmalade (except those sweetened with saccharine). He stipulates only a *small* helping a day of bananas, apples and sausages (except those made without bread or cereal); and as *much* as you like of bacon, ham, pork, kidneys, liver, meats of all kinds, poultry, fish of all kinds, especially herring, salmon, mackerel and sardines, almost all vegetables, salads, cheese and especially cream cheese, butter, cream, milk (but not more than ½ pint daily), eggs, meat fat, lard, dripping, olive oil, sunflower oil, unsaturated margarine. Coffee without sugar, black or with cream or a little milk, tea with lemon or a dash of milk, or water with or without unsweetened lemon juice—any quantity of these at every meal. No beer. Wine but it must be dry such as Claret, Chablis or dry white Bordeaux.

Mackarness finishes by quoting a menu for a whole food diet for weight reduction and good health that appeared in *Harper's and Queen*. You begin with the juice of one lemon in a glass of warm water, then yogurt sprinkled with 1 teaspoon wheat germ and 1 tablespoon bran, fresh fruit such as apple, pear, grapes, pineapple, melon, decaffeinated coffee, black or with skim milk.

Gaylord Hauser—famous for so long, admired (and listened to) by Garbo—is over eighty and doesn't look it. For years he's been advocating his way of eating: "only fresh, living food . . . enjoyed at times when you can relax . . . in surroundings that you love best." Not long ago British *Vogue* (October 1, 1975) checked things out with him once again.

Some sayings from "Chairman" Hauser:

Watch your blood sugar level . . . to maintain your blood sugar level between meals, use protein foods . . . sunflower seeds, milk, cottage cheese, or a hard-boiled egg.

Eat a good breakfast—one or two eggs, a little Swiss cheese, some whole wheat toast, fruit, milk.

Retrain your appetite—People are afraid of eating a big breakfast because they are afraid of overweight. Fundamentally, reducing means to find out what your body tolerates, how much you can eat to be fit, and then retraining your appetite.

Never eat when you are emotionally upset.

And, wisest of all: *We are all different. We look different. Our blood pressures are different. Why should we follow the same diet? . . . Learn to know what your body needs and be your own nutritionist.*

Then there are the Weight Watchers.

The idea is to learn new eating habits. To stop eating too much food and that of poor nutritional value and high-calorie content. To do this one does not count calories—this has already been done in setting up the daily diet. High-calorie, low-nutrition foods are banned, so are others not easily measured which "encourage cheating." Three meals a day *must* be eaten, never skipped. Weight loss is slow but steady. Weight Watchers advise people to consult their doctors while participating in the program with periodic check-ups. The big idea is to learn to stop reaching for the wrong food.

As for breakfast—one fruit *must* be taken. There is a wide variety listed along with the proper quantity such as "grapefruit ½ medium" or "orange juice 4 fluid ounces," "fresh frozen (unsweetened) or canned (unsweetened) packed in own juice. Freeze-dried may be used if equated to fresh fruit."

Eggs or cheese for breakfast: not more than 4 eggs per week—cooked in shell, poached or scrambled as directed. Not more than 4 ounces of hard cheese weekly. Consult your menu.

Bread: white, whole wheat or brown where indicated on menu plan. Slice should weigh no more than 1 ounce.

Milk: skimmed milk or skimmed milk powder or granules mixed with water.

No bacon, butter, cream, fried foods, fruits dried or canned in syrup, jams or preserves, pancakes, waffles, raw fish or meat, sardines, smoked fish, except salmon or haddock, soups, sugar, yogurt, syrups.

Morning Menu plan: juice or fruit; choice of hard cheese, 1 ounce (30 grams) *or* cottage cheese, 2 ounces (60 grams) *or* fish, 2 ounces (60 grams) *or* 1 egg, *or* cereal, 1 ounce (30 grams) with skimmed milk, 4 fluid ounces (1¼ demiliters); bread—1 slice for women and teenagers, 2 slices for men; beverage if desired (tea, coffee and other "legal" beverages can be taken any time).

At the common leveling-off point when it becomes harder to continue losing weight, a new plan is introduced to help get over the depressing state. A shift in emphasis here and there, different things. Curiously, breakfast remains the same. Then, rather charmingly, forbidden foods are reintroduced over a long period through a Maintenance Plan. Things like cake and alcohol. The point being to learn to *control* the intake of such foods. If trouble results you are advised to go back to the main program and begin again.

Drs. William F. Kremen and Laura Kremen, quoted in *Cosmopolitan* (November 1975), take a very different view of breakfast from any of the foregoing. According to them you wake up after not having done anything, so you're "still full of calories." They feel, especially if you are overweight, that "breakfast is the worst way to start the day." They observe, "not a single study has ever been published proving that one should eat upon rising, nor that one should eat three meals a day, nor that one should eat every day of the week." As for not working on an empty stomach—"That is sheer nonsense. You can work a lot better when your stomach is empty than when it is full." Far better, the good doctors say, to do some exercises, take a shower to get your circulation going—and you'll have gotten rid of some of those stored calories. You could call it "breaksleep." Orange juice? Cheaper and better to take a 500 mg tablet of vitamin C. As for cereals and such, the doctors agree with Dr. Mackarness about what happens to the sugar-using and producing process. Eggs and bacon? Great protein suppliers, *but* unfortunately, protein in combination with fat or starch and fat. Cottage cheese is almost pure protein and water—so is egg white alone. Go ahead and eat protein-plus-fat if you want but don't let it stimulate your appetite. Fresh fruit is okay—as much as you like, except bananas (high calories). Certain cheeses are all right. Fish. The doctors recommend tea very highly, but tea without sugar *or* honey. Chinese "green" tea is very good to drink "as is." Lemon can be added. They feel that milk, of course, is *"true* nutrition." Dilute milk with equal amount of water for adults. It tastes better than defatted milk and it goes twice as far. Buttermilk is good too. A little butter is permitted or one of the vegetable-fat margarines.

Their parting shot—breakfast "causes a big shift of circulating blood to the intestines, at the expense of blood circulation in the brain and muscle."

To extend possibilities just a little more, here is the breakfast part of a vegetarian menu from the *Guardian* (January 29, 1976) suggested by actress Morag Hood:

DAY ONE *porridge, banana, milk.*
DAY TWO *porridge, milk.*
DAY THREE *dates, toast, butter, marmite.*
DAY FOUR *orange, toast, butter, marmite.*
DAY FIVE *stewed apple, toast, butter, marmite.*
DAY SIX *porridge, milk.*
DAY SEVEN *toast, banana.*

And a "new basic breakfast" from the London *Times* (March 13, 1976)—home-made Muesli: Mix 2 ounces rolled oats, 1 ounce soft brown sugar, 1 ounce seedless raisins and 1 dessertspoon wheat germ in a bowl. To serve, measure out 3 tablespoons in a bowl. Add natural yogurt or milk and allow to soak for 5 minutes. Serve. You can add chopped apple or sliced banana or stewed fruit; more raisins.

Any contradictions that appear among these various "beliefs" are purely to be expected.

Tea

Many of the things said about coffee can be said about tea in the way of individual tastes and degrees and kinds of addiction. Still, tea is Another Thing. Its image is connected most of all with England and India, China and Japan, with milk or with lemon, unsweetened or sugared, or perhaps with honey. Mostly it's made in one, very simple way. Oh, these days there's powdered and bagged, but the best way is in a teapot—chipped stoneware or family silver—with a tea cozy hugging it warm.

Method: Fill kettle with fresh water and put on fire. Heat teapot. As kettle starts to boil put leaves in pot—about 1 small teaspoon per person (add 1 teaspoon for pot). When the water reaches its boiling point pour it over leaves. Let pot stand in warm place for three minutes or longer depending on the tea. If it infuses too long, tannin develops, causing the tea to become bitter. Pour slowly into warm cups, straining if desired. Having first poured milk (if you are taking it) into cup. Sweeten.

Tea comes from an evergreen bush of the Camellia family. It grows best high up and requires a warm, wet climate. These days the largest amount of it comes from India. China, where it all began, is ironically second and consumes the greater part of her production internally. Ceylon is third and Japan fourth. After that comes the USSR, Kenya, Indonesia, other parts of Africa, Turkey, Iran and Argentina. China, Japan and Taiwan chiefly produce green tea.

Legend has it that a Chinese emperor five thousand years ago was in the habit of boiling his drinking water. One day some leaves fell into it and he was delighted by the scent and the taste. We know there was tea drinking in China in the sixth century, and in 780 A.D. the first book about tea was written, the *Ch'a Ching*. By the ninth century Japan had taken it up and began to evolve the extraordinary tea ceremony still practiced today. The first tea to reach Europe was brought by the Dutch by way of Java in 1610.

The name *tea* derives from the Chinese *t'e* or *tcha* in the Cantonese dialect, therefore the colloquial expression (via India) "a cup of cha." When the Portuguese Princess Catharine of Braganza married King Charles II she brought chests of tea with her and set the fashion for tea drinking in the court. There were already coffee houses in England and Samuel Pepys, ever ready to try something new, wrote in the 1660s, "did send for a cupp of (a China drink) Tee which I had never drank before." Coffee

was soon ousted from its popularity and by 1750 tea became the principal drink of all British classes.

As always, there were those against it, who thought it bad for the health. But a distinguished Dutch physician, Dr. Cornelius Bontekoe, published a book in 1679 advocating drinking eight to ten cups a day or as many as a hundred or more which he claimed he drank himself!

Tea is vulnerable to moisture and odors which it absorbs. Therefore it is important to store it in a dry place, away from strong-smelling things like spices, cooking oils or disinfectants. It should be kept in an air-tight tin or tea caddy (the word derives from *catty*—an Oriental measure of weight). A cup of tea contains a little under one grain of caffeine on the average. As it is drunk, the caffeine is released gradually and its stimulus comes about fifteen minutes later.

A haunting legend about the origin of tea and its stimulating properties is repeated by Desfontaines: "Darma, a very pious prince, and son of an Indian king, landed in China in the year 510 of the Christian era, and wishing to edify mankind by his example, imposed upon himself privations of all kinds. It happened, however, that after several years of great fatigue, in spite of his care he fell asleep; and believing he had violated his oath, and in order to fulfill it faithfully for the future, he cut off his eyelids and threw them on the ground. The next day, returning towards the same spot, he found them

changed into a little shrub, hitherto unknown on earth. He ate some of the leaves, which made him merry and restored his former strength. Having recommended the same food to his disciples, the reputation of tea soon spread, and has continued in use since that time."

This would seem to be backed up by Dr. Thomas Short who wrote his *Discourse on Tea* in 1750: "What should mightily recommend the use of Tea to Gentlemen of a sprightly Genius, who would preserve the Continuance of their lively and distinct ideas, is its eminent and unequalled Power to take off, or prevent, Drowsiness and Dullness, Damps and Clouds on the Brain, and intellectual Faculties. It begets a watchful Briskness, dispels Heaviness: it keeps the Eyes wakeful, the Head clear, animates the intellectual Powers, maintains or raises lively ideas, excites and sharpeneth the Thoughts, gives fresh Vigour and Force to Invention, awakens the Senses and clears the Mind."

Even so the food historian Reay Tannahill does not find it easy to understand why tea became the favorite drink of the British people: "It cannot have been because it was filling; coffee and chocolate are far more satisfying drinks. It cannot have been because it was cheap; coffee and chocolate were both much cheaper. It cannot have been because people thought tea nourishing; doctors and politicians pointed out, frequently and vocally (and truthfully), that beer was far more nourishing."

Alexis Soyer wrote in *Pantropheon* (1853) that "There are, in reality, but two kinds of tea, black tea and green tea; each kind is again subdivided into many varieties. The best black tea is the scented *Liang-sing*. . . . The first of all green teas, destined for the great, and bearing on exquisite perfume, is that called *Koo-lang-fyn-i*."

Whittard's of London, typical of the finest tea and coffee merchants, list a number of teas from Darjeeling, Ceylon, Assam; a half-dozen tisanes or herbal teas; teas like Lapsang Souchong from China along with Keemun, Chingwo, scented Pekoes, Rose Petal, Earl Grey, Formosa Oolong, and green teas like Formosa Gunpowder, Chunmee, and Moyune Gunpowder. Here is a list of some of their teas:

Darjeeling Teas most delicately flavored of Indian teas, rich, exquisite bouquet, reminiscent of Muscat.
Ceylon Teas from higher altitudes where quality is better.
Assam Teas from Northeast India, generally full, thick and rich.
Lapsang Souchong from South China, black with a slightly tarry or smoky flavor. A pinch adds a connoisseur's touch to any type of tea.
Keemun "Burgundies" of China teas, black, from the north, rich aroma and color.
Pelham Mixture blend of choice China teas, beautifully scented with Jasmine, Bergamot, etc., subtle, rich, distinctive.

Formosa Oolong semifermented, greenish brown tippy tea, natural, fruity flavor, pungent and piquant, much used for blending.

Green Teas name given to unfermented teas, excellent drunk without milk or sugar during rich, heavy meal.

And here are several more described by the Tea Council:

Nilgiris from southern India, delicate in flavor, bright.

Dimbula high-grown tea from Ceylon, fine flavor, golden.

Kandy full-bodied from Ceylon, full flavored, strong colored.

Nuwara Eliya from Ceylon, famous light bright color, fragrant.

Uva from eastern slopes of Ceylon, fine flavor.

> "[I am] a hardened and shameless tea drinker, who has for many years diluted his meals with only the infusion of this fascinating plant: whose kettle has scarcely time to cool: who with tea amuses the evening, with tea solaces the midnight and with tea welcomes the morning . . ."
>
> *Dr. Johnson*

A tea-tasting held at a shop in Caernarvon, Wales, about the year 1916.

Children's Hour

The American writer Naomi Lazard says that breakfast is the only edible meal in England because it is a children's meal and the English are fixated at that level. Well, true or not, there is a sense of comforting familiarity about breakfast in the minds of children of whatever age the world over. And this is reflected in children's stories and poems.

A. A. Milne, to take a celebrated example, deals with breakfast in *The House at Pooh Corner*. Tigger appears in the middle of the night at Pooh Bear's house, and the next morning Pooh offers him honey for breakfast. Tigger tries it and decides that Tiggers don't like it. So Pooh offers to take him round to Piglet's place for some haycorns. "Thank you, Pooh," said Tigger, "because haycorns is really what Tiggers like best." Tigger is asked not to be "too bouncy." To which he replies that Tiggers are only bouncy before breakfast but as soon as they have a few haycorns they become "Quiet and Refined." Piglet thereupon gives Tigger a bowl of haycorns. Tigger munches away for a bit then excuses himself and goes out. He returns to announce that, "Tiggers don't like haycorns." So they try thistles. At the suggestion, Tigger responds with his refrain—"Thistles is what Tiggers like best." And of course Tiggers turn out not to like thistles at all. They meet up with Eeyore and Kanga and Christopher Robin. Eeyore thinks Kanga is "sure to have lots of breakfast" for Tigger. But Tigger doesn't like anything in her cupboard. What

it turns out he *does* like is Roo's Extract of Malt medicine, which he discovers by licking the spoon. *That's* what all Tiggers like. So he decides to live there.

Then there is a certain Miss Muffet:

> Little Miss Muffet
> Sat on a tuffet
> Eating her curds and whey;
> There came a big spider,
> Who sat down beside her
> And frightened Miss Muffet away.

Another famous tale goes as follows:

Once upon a time there were Three Bears who lived in a house in a wood. One of them was a Baby Bear and one was a Momma Bear and one was a Great, Big, Papa Bear. And they each had a bowl for their porridge: a little bowl for Baby Bear, a middle-sized bowl for Momma Bear, and a great, big bowl for Papa Bear.

One day after they had made the porridge for their breakfast and poured it into their porridge bowls, they decided to take a walk in the woods to let the porridge cool so they wouldn't burn their mouths by trying to eat it too soon. And while they were out, Goldilocks appeared . . .

As everyone knows, Goldilocks was a bit of a busy-body and on this occasion she ended up exploring the Bears' home. She also ended up eating all of Baby Bear's porridge which was "just right" after she had tried Papa Bear's (too hot) and Momma Bear's (too cold). Next she tested all the chairs for some reason and again Baby Bear's chair was predictably "just right." But somehow she broke the seat. This didn't deter her, however, from going upstairs to discover the bedroom. In a rut as she was, she tried all three beds in diminishing size and found Baby Bear's "just right." And she went to sleep in it.

The Bears meanwhile, who should have had more sense about how long it takes for porridge to get cold, returned home. Goldilocks—never one for manners—had left the spoon in Papa Bear's bowl and he exclaimed on seeing it, "Someone's been eating *my* porridge!" Momma Bear found the same situation and said the same thing, "Someone's been eating *my* porridge!" Good son that he was, Baby Bear found *his* all gone and said, "Someone's been eating *my* porridge, and it's all gone!"

This leads us to the chairs and similar repetitions, and then to the upstairs and to the bedroom and similar repetitions, until Baby Bear—no fool when it comes to believing his eyes—sees a little girl in his bed and cries, "Someone's been lying in *my* bed and here she is!"

Goldilocks hadn't heard a thing throughout all this, of course, but she heard Baby Bear all right! And quite sensibly, confronted with three totally strange bears, she jumped up and jumped out of the window (from the second floor, mind you) and ran away.

"There's no use trying," she said: "one can't believe impossible things."

"I dare say you haven't had much practice," said the Queen. "When I was your age, I always did it for half-an-hour a day. Why, sometimes I believed as many as six impossible things before breakfast."

from THROUGH THE LOOKING-GLASS
by Lewis Carroll

One of Wedgwood's delightful set of dishes especially designed for children's breakfast. This one is decorated with scenes from Alice in Wonderland.

On the Page

The novelist and memoir writer has the advantage over the playwright or film-maker of being able to tell us outright what his or her characters are thinking as they go about their actions. True, the screenwriter can give us a kind of interior monologue, but this is always pretty self-conscious in effect.

I have chosen four works in which breakfast figures—all, coincidentally, written by women. All are worlds apart. One reveals breakfast as a kind of family trial with father as judge; one is a hilarious spoof of the novel as High Romance; one is about a young woman full of sadness and narcissism; one an ecstatic recollection of childhood.

The curiously original English novelist Ivy Compton-Burnett who tells her stories primarily in dialogue and a stylized speech which allows truths to strike like daggers, uses breakfast again and again throughout her book *A House and Its Head* (1935). In the three scenes represented here she shows us the morning meal as a combination trial and judgment, a place of questions and perilous answers. The book opens like a play: "The day was Christmas Day in the year eighteen eighty-four, and the room was the usual dining room of an eighteenth century country house. . . ." Duncan Edgeworth, the "head" of the novel's title, is waiting with his wife, Ellen, for their children to appear. " 'The children are late, are they not,' said Ellen, to whom speech clearly ranked above silence." She goes on, " 'I

think there are more presents than usual. Oh, I wish they would all come down.' " Duncan asks, " 'Why do you wish it?' "

The scene continues as follows:

"Well, it is not a day when we want them to be late, is it?"

"Do we want them to be late on any day? Oh, of course, it is Christmas Day. I saw the things on the table."

[And on and on it goes until Ellen says she hears a sound on the stairs.]

"A sound on the stairs! A remarkable thing to hear at this time of morning!"

"It is Nance; I know her step. I am glad that one of them is down."

"Glad? Why?"

(Ellen gives no reason.)

"It is a natural thing for a young woman to come downstairs in the morning to have her breakfast," said Duncan, seeing to disclaim any less tangent purpose in his daughter. "Well, Nance, you have condescended to join us?"

When asked if she has seen anything of Grant and Sibyl, the other young people, her retort rings many familiar bells as to how people feel first thing in the morning: " 'No, Father. It is not a time of day when family intercourse flourishes.' " These repetitive questions and sarcastic or ironic or cruelly true answers continue, through the mouths of the characters and the marvelous acid commentary of the author, to tell us the story. The others in their turn come down—to much the same parry and thrust.

In Chapter IX we read of a similar situation where Duncan finds himself waiting for someone to come down to breakfast, only this time it is Alison, his brand new wife—Ellen has died. The question of sending her up a tray is raised, whereupon she appears, to say candidly, to say the least, " 'Oh, now I begin this sitting in someone else's place!' "

Chapter X finds news of the birth of a baby to Duncan and Alison—only we know it is by Duncan's nephew Grant. A friend rushes around the neighborhood to spread the news, beginning ridiculously at the house of Dr. Smollett who *delivered* the baby in the early morning. When she is asked to stay for breakfast she replies that she believes she will: " 'I left home after such a very light meal, to be betimes with my news; and now I find it is not news, I am conscious of an emptiness.' " At one point she cries, " 'By Jove, these mushrooms are what they ought to be!' " but when she hears that word is being spread by the boy who delivers the milk, she rises saying, " 'That determines my interlude for sustenance, I am not going to be anticipated by boys from farms.' "

Stella Gibbons, in her altogether hilarious novel *Cold Comfort Farm*, has taken the precaution of starring the best passages. For as she writes in a foreword, "I have adopted the method perfected by the late Herr Baedeker, and firmly marked what I consider the finer passages with one, two or three stars. In such a manner did the good man deal with cathedrals, hotels and paintings by men of genius. There seems no reason why it should not be applied to passages in novels.

"It ought to help reviewers too."

Chapter III gets two stars. It begins: "Dawn crept over the Downs like a sinister white animal . . ." and contains sensual, even erotic references to breakfast.

Such as: "In the large kitchen, which occupied most of the middle of the house, a sullen fire burned, the smoke of which wavered up the blackened walls and over the deal table, darkened by age and dirt, which was roughly set for a meal. A snood full of coarse porridge hung over the fire, and standing with one arm resting upon the high mantel, looking moodily down into the heaving contents of the snood, was a tall young man whose riding-boots were splashed with mud to the thigh, and whose coarse linen shirt was open to his waist. The firelight lit up his diaphragm muscles as they heaved slowly in rough rhythm with the porridge.

"He looked up as Judith entered, and gave a short, defiant laugh, but said nothing. Judith slowly crossed over until she stood by his side. She was tall as he. They stood in silence, she staring at him, and he down into the secret crevasses of the porridge.

" 'Well, mother mine,' he said at last, 'here I am, you see. I said I would be in time for breakfast, and I have kept my word.'

"His voice had a low, throaty, animal quality, a sneering warmth that wound a velvet ribbon of sexuality over the outward coarseness of the man.

"Judith's breath came in long shudders. She thrust her arms deeper into her shawl. The porridge gave an ominous, leering heave; it might almost have been endowed with life, so uncannily did its movements keep pace with the human passions that throbbed above it."

A totally different effect is brilliantly achieved by the recently rediscovered English novelist Jean Rhys. She began publishing under the sponsorship of Ford Madox Ford in 1927, and stopped, after five books, in 1939. Then, in the sixties, *Wide Sargasso Sea*, her extraordinary, imaginative evocation of the first Mrs. Rochester from Charlotte Brontë's *Jane Eyre*, appeared to great acclaim. Since then, nearly all of her work has been reissued. Her world of hung-over, sexually promiscuous girls in London and Paris during the first half of this century, has about it something of a wild mixture of Colette, Sally Bowles, D. H. Lawrence, the paintings of Walter Sickert, Raymond Chandler, Hemingway and Scott Fitzgerald. She seems, through her clear, self-pitiless gaze, her glimpses of tropic sunlight and foliage (she was born in the Caribbean), often more modern than they.

In her first novel, *Voyage in the Dark*, she tells of the decline and fall of a young woman, a chorus girl in a touring company who ends up in a friend's flat suffering complications from an abortion. About halfway through the book, Walter, the man Anna has been having an affair with, is leaving London and, she realizes sadly, her. Their last night she falls very ill and he puts her into a taxi:

When I got home I lay down without undressing. Then it got light and I thought that when Mrs. Dawes came in with my breakfast she would think I had gone mad. So I got up and undressed.

She spends most of her days lying in bed till very late, eating her first meal in bed and taking long baths in the afternoon. Then one day:

I felt ill when I woke up. I had pains all over me. I lay there and after a while I heard the landlady coming up the stairs . . . "It's gone ten," she said. "I'm a bit late this morning with your breakfast but my clock stopped. This came for you; a messenger-boy brought it."

There was a letter on the breakfast-tray, and a big bunch of violets. I took them up; they smelt like rain.

The landlady was watching me with her little red eyes. I said, "Can I have my hot water?"

and she went out. I opened the letter and there were five five-pound notes inside.

She remembers her awful stepmother Hester jawing away at Morgan's Rest and having to listen to her talking about Cambridge and England. They are having breakfast at half-past twelve:

We ate fishcakes and sweet potatoes and then we had guavas; and bread-fruit instead of bread because she liked to feel she was eating bread-fruit.

Sitting there eating you could see the curve of a hill like the curve of a green shoulder. And there were pink roses on the table in a curly blue vase with gold rings.

At another point her landlady *does* find her still dressed from the night before:

When Mrs. Dawes came in with breakfast I was lying on the bed with all my clothes on. I hadn't even taken off my shoes. She didn't say anything, she didn't look surprised, and when she looked at me I knew she was thinking, "There you are. I always knew this would happen." I imagined I saw her smile as she turned away.

After a horrendous night out with a girl friend later in the story, they go to the girl friend's flat. Anna has behaved badly and is on the defensive:

We got to Berners Street and went upstairs.
The old woman came to the door to meet us.
"Shall I get breakfast, miss?"

The formality of many family breakfasts and the isolation of individuals is perfectly captured in this illustration from Cassell's Family Magazine *(England, 1878).*

"Yes," Laurie said, "and turn a bath on, hurry up."

I stood in the passage. She went into the bedroom and brought my dress out.

"Here's your dress," she said. "And for God's sake don't look like that. Come on and have something to eat."

She kissed me all of a sudden.

"Oh, come on," she said. "I'm a good old cow really. You know I'm fond of you. To tell you the truth I was a bit screwed last night too. You can pretend to be a virgin for the rest of your life as far as I'm concerned; I don't care. What's it got to do with me?"

"Don't start a speech," I said, "I've got a splitting headache. Have a heart."

It was the first fine day for weeks. The old woman spread a white cloth on the table in the sitting-room and the sun shone on it. Then she went into the kitchen and started to fry bacon. There was the smell of the bacon and the sound of the water running into the bath. And nothing else. My head felt empty.

Later she moves in with a masseuse and feels that maybe things will be better. Again she remembers her childhood:

She'll smile and put the tray down and I'll say . . . I've had such an awful dream—it was only a dream she'll say—and on the tray the blue cup and saucer and the silver teapot so I'd know for certain it had started again my lovely life—like a five-finger exercise played very slowly on the piano like a garden with a high wall round it—and every now and again thinking I only dreamt it it never happened.

But true to form she has a terrific fight with the masseuse, who eventually apologizes:

"Poor kid," she said, blinking at me. "You don't look well and that's a fact. I'll bring you up some breakfast.". . .

"Thanks," I said. "Just some tea—not anything to eat."

I kept telling myself, "You've got to make a plan." But instead I started counting all the towns I had been to, the first winter I was on tour . . . all the bedrooms on tour. Always a high, dark wardrobe and something dirty red in the room; and through the window the feeling of a small street would come in. And the breakfast-tray dumped down on the bed, two plates with a bit of curled-up bacon on each . . .

One night when she comes back to the flat with a man, the masseuse is discreetly out and Anna starts singing:

Oh, I bet my money on the bob-tailed nag,
Somebody won on the bay,
   and he said, "It's 'Somebody bet on the bay'."
   I said, "I'll sing it how I like it. Somebody won on the bay."

It could serve as her motto and epitaph.

I am not alone in thinking Colette's remembrances of her mother, *Sido* and *My Mother's House*, among her greatest works. Somehow their profound debt to love is paid with radiant insight and poetry. In one section of the latter Colette describes her mother this way:

At five o'clock in the morning I would be awakened by the clank of a full bucket being set down in the kitchen sink immediately opposite my room.

"What are you doing with the bucket, mother? Couldn't you wait until Josephine arrives?"

And out I hurried. But the fire was already blazing, fed with dry wood. The milk boiling on the blue-tiled charcoal stove. Nearby, a bar of chocolate was melting in a little water for my breakfast, and, seated squarely in her cane armchair, my mother was grinding the fragrant coffee which she roasted herself. The morning hours were kind to her. She wore their rosy colors in her cheeks. Flushed with a brief return to health, she would gaze at the rising sun, while the church bell rang for early Mass. . . . At seventy-one dawn still found her undaunted, if not always undamaged. Burnt by the fire, cut with the pruning knife, soaked by melting snow or spilt water, she had always managed to enjoy her best moments of independence before the earliest risers had opened their shutters. She was able to tell us of the cat's awakening, of what was going on in the nests, of news gleaned, together with the morning's milk and the warm loaf, from the milk-maid and the baker's girl, the record in fact of the birth of a new day.

It was not until one morning when I found the kitchen unwarmed and the blue enamel saucepan hanging on the wall, that I felt my mother's end to be near. Her illness knew many respites, during which the fire flared up again on the hearth, and the smell of fresh bread and melting chocolate stole under the door together with the cat's impatient paw. . . . My brother, returning before sunrise from attending a distant patient, one day caught my mother red-handed in the most wanton of crimes. Dressed in her nightgown, but wearing heavy gardening sabots, her little gray septuagenarian's plait of hair turning up like a scorpion's tail on the nape of her neck, one foot firmly planted on the crosspiece of the beech trestle, her back bent in the attitude of the expert jobber, my mother, rejuvenated by an indescribable expression of guilty enjoyment, in defiance of all her promises and of the freezing morning dew, was sawing logs in her own yard.

Trains and Boats and Planes

> "I assure you Mr. Player was wrong in supposing that I thought you purchased inferior coffee. I thought I said to him I was surprised you should buy such bad roasted *corn*. I did not believe you had such a thing as coffee in the place: I am certain I never tasted any . . ."
>
> *Isambard Kingdom Brunel in a letter to the caterer of the British Rail Buffet at Swindon station*

There can be a tremendous poetry to trains and ships, less so to planes, although I imagine flying to the Orient on the pre-war Pan American Clipper must have been pretty poetic and Concorde has a certain poetry of speed. I take my title from the poetry of popular song—Bert Bacharach's haunting tune. Trains had and have marvelous names—Santa Fe Chief, Twentieth Century Limited, Zephyr, Orient-Express, North Star, Flying Scot, Brighton Belle,★ Golden Arrow. The famed Pullman sleeping cars and dining cars were named. So were engines. In Europe the legendary Wagon-Lits carried kings, maharajahs, millionaires and spies. One could go to

★ A train on which Laurence Olivier was a regular traveler. A story goes that one morning Lord Olivier noticed that kippers were not on the menu. So outraged was he that he wrote to *The Times*. In due course, kippers were restored to the menu. The funny part of the story occurred sometime later when Lord Olivier was asked by a smiling waiter if he wished kippers, only to be answered benignly, "No thank you. Bacon and eggs." He didn't necessarily want the kippers, just the choice.

Cairo or Peking, to Constantinople or Oslo. When the Calais-Méditerrannée began its service to the Riviera the marvelous deep blue color of the cars caused the public to rename it the "*Train Bleu*." They gave another name to another train, or rather one of its cars: a private one belonging to Léopold II, King of the Belgians, who liked to entertain the dancer Cléo de Mérode on board. They dubbed it "Cléopold."

There is no doubt that the most famous train of all, the Paris to Istanbul Orient-Express, was extraordinary. It too was given wonderful names: "*Le roi des trains et le train des rois*" was one. "*Le rapide de la mort*" was another. A rather sad descendant of that fabled train still goes from Paris to Istanbul via the route further south adapted after the war. It travels via Milan, Venice, Trieste, Belgrade and Sofia and is called the Simplon-Orient-Express. Journalists and others who have tried it lately have sad tales to tell—of lack of food or beverages, endless delays, shabby interiors, of being locked in their compartments in certain countries. Brigid Keenan and Ian Jack of the London *Sunday Times* reported in January 1976 that there was no restaurant car at all and no real breakfast. At one point they were served instant coffee in plastic cups and a tray of biscuits. I still would like to try it.

My own memories of trains are guaranteed to cause nostalgia: winding slowly through the Rocky Mountains in heavy snow in the direction of the sunset and San Francisco, eating and drinking to the sound of Billie Holliday singing the blues; standing up all the way from Chicago to New York during wartime; searching out an ancestral place called Berry Pomeroy in Devon by means of a whole series of country trains with the old individual compartments you entered from either side that had no access to each other; a long, delicious meal hurtling southward from Rome to Naples; a magical journey along the Riviera into Italy with the sun-dazzled Mediterranean on my right. An endless trip from Barcelona to Madrid that taught me something about the actual size of Spain. Going to Los Angeles from San Francisco on the old Southern Pacific.

Railroads have found themselves in great difficulty—all over the world. They are losing enormous sums of money. Many of the most famous ones in America have gone bankrupt. Happily, hopeful from my point of view, there are those who want them saved—saved and even improved. The French have been trying to replace their vast losses during World War II. Modern methods, new trains are being experimented with and taken up. British Rail is aiming toward high-speed service for long distances. In the United States the new, amalgamated services are called Amtrak and they are fighting very hard to re-establish something of the comfort and pleasure traveling by train can mean.

One of the things I've always loved about trains is the fact they deliver you right in the heart of your destination. Another is the freedom to roam from car to car, to go to the club or bar car for a drink, or to the dining car for a meal. Not very long ago I had occasion to try breakfast on an English train traveling from London in the direction of Cambridge. It was a Saturday morning and I had time to order breakfast before getting to my destination, Audley End. It was a confusing experience but with a happy ending. I entered the restaurant car which was not a formal diner but had a service bar at one end and a series of small tables and chairs along both sides. There was no sign of a menu for breakfast and none was offered by the pleasant and efficient waiter in his attractive red jacket. A printed card on each table simply read: "Saloon Service: Cup of Coffee and Biscuits, 26p; Pot of Tea and Biscuits, 30p." At the bottom was the nice new phrase of British Rail, "Travellers-Fare." I ordered coffee. When it arrived it was poured at the same time as hot milk into my cup. I noticed on the biscuit tray that there were two pieces of buttered toast. "I'll have that," I said cheerfully. It was warm, well buttered, and there was a jar (not a plastic container) of Robertson's Golden Shred marmalade on a saucer. My table, by the way, was covered with a clean white cloth and I had a linen napkin. On the table were Colman's English Mustard, salt, pepper, sugar cubes. The china was a blue-gray stoneware.

The mustard made me wonder and the next time the man came round with more coffee/hot milk, I

decided to ask if they served a proper breakfast. "Oh, yes, sir," was the reply. And then, very English, by way of forewarning, "It'll be two pounds, sir." That's about four dollars. His not having "pushed" breakfast when I first sat down suggested to me his slight embarrassment at the recent rise in the cost of breakfast from £1.60 to £2. But being curious, and hungry, I asked him to bring me some. This was somewhat odd too as still no menu was forthcoming. The waiter asked me if I wanted fruit or tomato juice. I had the latter. It was chilled and served on a saucer with a paper doily on it. When my main dish came it was piping hot and beautifully cooked: one egg, sunny-side-up on fried bread; two tomatoes, grilled; two rashers of bacon; one sausage; button mushrooms (canned, however); three slices of toast (warm) and lots of butter. If British Rail can equal that standard of preparation and service elsewhere (to be fair, I was the only person having a full meal at the time), the celebrated "English Breakfast" is in no danger.

If I'd been offered a menu it would have listed other things such as porridge, corn flakes, sautéed potatoes, fried bread, grilled kippers or poached haddock.

A 1920 breakfast menu on the Alaska Railroad makes me yearn for the Good Old Days. Fruits offered include fresh oranges, grapefruit, pineapple, prunes (stewed), casabas, bananas, peaches, apple sauce and baked apples; "any cereal"; fried halibut with tartar sauce or Alaska trout, to order; chops, steaks, reindeer steak, ham, sausages, eggs any way, hash; griddle cakes, French toast, milk toast, Boston cream toast, French pancakes; pie; doughnuts, cookies, hot rolls, toast, butter and jams. Not to mention "Royal Corona Coffee"; "Ceylon, English Breakfast or Green Tea"; coffee or chocolate by the pot; milk by the bottle.

In contrast the present Amtrak menu offers: an "eye opener" Bloody Mary or Screwdriver; Continental Breakfast of chilled fruit juice, warmed Danish pastry; coffee, tea, or milk; Club Breakfast of five choices: chilled juice, French toast with butter and syrup, ham or bacon or sausage, coffee, tea, milk; juice, two eggs "as you like them," ham or bacon sausage, toast or muffin, butter and jelly, beverage; juice, buttermilk pancakes with butter and syrup, ham or sausage or bacon, beverage; juice, one egg "as you like it," toast, butter and jelly, beverage; juice, "fluffy" three-egg omelette filled with jelly or cheese, ham or bacon or sausage, toast or muffin, butter and jelly, beverage. These appear to be the standard dishes for the entire system. This one is for the Southwest Ltd. The Lake Shore Ltd. omits the fifth choice. There is also an attractive menu for "young travelers under 12" which contains two offerings: "The Baggage Car"—two scrambled eggs with bacon, toast and jelly, milk, and "The Silver Spike"—pancakes with bacon and fried egg, whipped butter, maple syrup, milk.

OPPOSITE: *In the 1870s cooking on the Great Northern Railway in England was done in the open air and the dining-car accommodations were truly elaborate.*

PHOTO—JEAN-CLAUDE DEWOLF

Breakfast on a French train without croissants *would be a contradiction in terms.*

These days the French offer a number of options. Aside from the classic restaurant car there is a "Grill-Express" with hot dishes available for self-service like an automat (and quite surprisingly good). Something referred to as "plateau service" which is like an airplane with trays served to passengers in their seats on drop-down tables. Of course the French continue their tradition of the anti-breakfast breakfast. The menu lists: fruit juice; coffee, tea, chocolate or Nescafé; toast, *brioche*, *croissant*; butter and jams. There *is* as well an *à la carte* menu offering eggs, ham, bacon, cheese, yogurt, fruit, etc., along with beers, wines and mineral waters. I've not yet eaten a morning meal on the superb "Mistral" that runs from Paris to Nice, but having had a glorious lunch on it, I hope to. I still can't forget the soft colors of the decoration and the glass doors between coaches that slide silently open as you approach.

As for boats, ships more properly, my own experiences differ widely—from cafeteria-style breakfasts on a reconverted troop ship full of students sailing to England in 1947 to first class on the *Leonardo da Vinci* out of Genoa bound for New York. By now there should be no need, I hope, to repeat endlessly the fruit juice, cereal, eggs and bacon, coffee or tea formula. I will simply point out variations and differences. One thing about first class on the Italian line is the total luxury of not having to consult a menu. One simply ordered whatever one wanted—from caviar to steak—and got it, warmly and well served—if they had it.

When the United States line's ships were still crossing and recrossing the Atlantic—alas, America no longer boasts even one transatlantic liner—a typical menu on, say, the *Independence* or *Constitution* included melon in season, frozen strawberries or peaches, fresh pineapple, pears, apple juice; broiled kippered herring; Créole omelette; corned beef hash with green peppers; Yorkshire ham; boiled or hashed brown potatoes; cheeses; cold smoked sausages; buckwheat griddle cakes; bagels, zwieback; milk and melba toast; honey. Other menus list baked codfish cakes with tomato sauce; creamed chipped beef on toast; fresh strawberries; baked apple; grapes; sauerkraut or clam juice; preserved figs, cherries or kumquats; steamed salt mackerel with celery butter; chicken livers; omelettes with shrimp or veal kidneys; tripe with rice; lamb chops, steak, Wesfalian ham, cold breast of chicken, beefsteak tartare; waffles, English muffins, Scotch scones, currant buns; "Kusch Kusch Demi Glace," Neufchâtel and Boursin; "Bacaboo con Papas" (young steer liver with Lyonnaise potatoes); "Frikadelle, Demi Glace."

The Peninsular and Oriental Steam Navigation Company, more popularly known as the P & O, has long been famous for, among other things, its breakfasts. People still talk of the days when Britishers commuted to the Far East by sea and the word "posh" evolved—port-side out, starboard home. P & O sail all over the world—to the Orient, to the Mediterranean, to the Caribbean and the North Sea. Continental breakfasts are served to passengers in their cabins or beside the swimming pool. In the ships' restaurants the typical menu offers, aside from the obvious, melon; pineapple juice; figs, apples and prunes; yogurt; kippered herrings, smoked had-

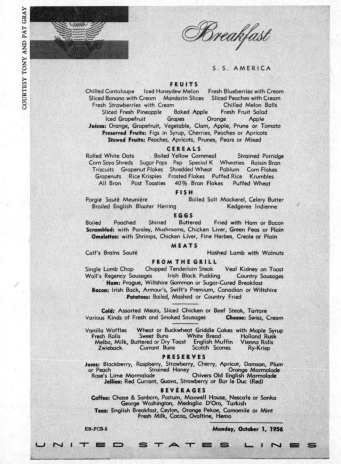

Those were the days : a breakfast menu from the erstwhile liner S.S. America, *dated October 1, 1956.*

dock; fried bread and grilled tomatoes.

Sad that of the last great liners only the *Queen Elizabeth II* now remains.

Flying is another story—a question of space (not very much) and time (sometimes very little) when it comes to meals. In my experience (I've never flown first class) breakfast tends to involve rubbery eggs disguised as "omelettes." I would think that things like cold meats or fish, cheeses, hard-boiled eggs, etc. would be much more edible. Way back in 1935 when Alice B. Toklas accompanied Gertrude Stein on her triumphal tour of America, she noted that when they took a plane (fairly glamorous in those days) from Fort Worth, Texas, to California, "the restaurant packed us a box of food that was the best picnic lunch there ever was. It would be a pleasure to be able to order something approaching it when taking a plane today [1954]. Has food on American planes—not the transatlantic flights but on interior routes—improved? It has not in Europe, it is incredibly bad, even worse than on trains. Do they cook these meals in the locomotive and in the fuselage?"

Well, I've had one or two pretty good dinners in the air, but never breakfast. United Airlines tries to get off to a good start by reproducing paintings of American scenes in full color on their menu covers—places like Telegraph Hill in San Francisco, the Water Tower in Chicago, Olvera Street in Los Angeles, Lexington Avenue and 62nd Street in New York, the White House in Washington, D.C., and the Koolau Mountains in Hawaii. The choice? Chilled pineapple chunks; Crepes à la Reine (creamed chicken filling), pork link sausages or French toast, syrup and sausages; blueberry muffin; creamery butter; beverages. Another menu varies the main dishes: Western omelette, grilled ham steak or Baked Eggs Paysanne with Ham; Danish roll, creamery butter. A typical first-class menu reads: fresh Grapefruit Supreme or chilled apricot halves in syrup; choice of Poached Eggs Benedict on English muffin with buttered asparagus or Crêpes à la Reine with Asparagus or grilled lamb chop, smoked ham steak or pork link sausages; *croissant* roll; coffee cake; butter curls; beverages.

Pan Am on one of its flights offers champagne or Bloody Mary; chilled fruit juices; fluffy cheese omelette; Eggs Benedict; grilled loin lamb chops; link sausages; hickory-smoked ham; home-fried potatoes; grilled tomato; selection of breakfast rolls, creamery butter, preserves; beverages. On a London-Frankfurt-Istanbul flight, aside from fruit, bread, preserves, and beverage, only a cheese omelette, Canadian bacon and grilled sausages are offered. From Karachi to New Delhi breakfast shrinks to Continental with only juices, breads and beverages. From New Delhi to Bangkok the only variation from the London-Istanbul flight is a choice of cheese omelette or one with diced tomatoes. On the Tokyo to San Francisco run, aside from the usual, grilled filet mignon and Poached Eggs Benedict plus grilled tomato are listed. The menus are beautifully illustrated in full color.

Alitalia hands out what can only be described as sensationally designed and printed menus with illustrations from the fifteenth-century *Tacuinum Sanitatis* (The Book of Health) or seventeenth-century wood engravings of kitchen utensils. Their *prima colazione*, or breakfast, between Bombay and Bangkok consists of the following: grapefruit segments; plain omelette, broiled lamb cutlets, crispy bacon; plum tomatoes; *croissants*; plus the usual juice, bread, preserves, beverages. Nairobi to Tananarive: sautéed mushrooms; tropical fruit salad; grilled noisettes of lamb. Rome to Bombay offers stuffed tomatoes. Different locations don't seem to bring about much change.

British Airways, which also gives out extremely attractive menus, offers first class, Miami-London: fresh fruit; yogurt; freshly scrambled or boiled eggs; grilled ham; tomatoes; mushrooms; fruit basket; breads; preserves; beverages. Tourist class gets: fruit; cold York ham with cheese, egg, tomato; bread, preserves, beverages. Nairobi to Zurich: Pineapple and melon slices; grilled bacon with chipolatas; and mushrooms are the variations.

Air Canada on long-haul flights serves their first-class passengers juices, fresh fruit cup; selection of omelettes; small breakfast steak, sausage and Canadian bacon; hash brown potatoes; selection of sweet and bread rolls; butter and preserves; beverage. On short hauls the steak is eliminated and the food is served on pre-set trays rather than from a cart. Economy class—aside from juice, etc.—has a main dish of two-egg omelette, $\frac{1}{2}$ tomato parmesan and Canadian bacon. Other flights offer things like broiled filet mignon, potato pancakes, scrambled eggs in tart shell, soft-boiled eggs in tomato cup and Spanish omelette.

I can't tell you what they serve for breakfast on Concorde because they don't serve breakfast. Not yet. The scheduled flights so far don't include those hours of the day. Which leads me to wonder whether or not there will be any time for food at all in the future with its faster and faster transport. A great many of us read of the nearly abstract rations given the astronauts—powdered this, packaged that. The better science-fiction writers and film makers haven't been too encouraging either: different-colored pills to simulate various food experiences. And in *Space Odyssey: 2001* food for some of the voyagers had become merely another part of their "life support system." Some people predict that not very long from now a trip as ordinary, say, as going from New York to Paris will be pretty much like getting in and out of a high-speed elevator—no time for a couple of drinks or a smoke, let alone champagne and orange juice and a bit of romance!

Marmalade

There are many marvelous jams, jellies, preserves and honeys that can adorn the breakfast plate, and there are innumerable excellent books dealing with them. But marmalade is surely so synonymous with breakfast that it deserves a chapter to itself. Its beautiful color and bittersweet taste seem just the thing to prepare for the day—full of promise but critical of false hopes; a kiss with a kick. Frances Fox Sandmel, in an article in the *Illustrated London News* (Christmas 1975), fully agrees: "If it has been used purely . . . the marmalade of memory should be associated with a particular time of day: morning. People who know agree that marmalade should be served only for breakfast."

There is the fantasy-history that relates how Mary Queen of Scots' Spanish doctor concocted marmalade in the 1560s to help overcome Her Majesty's seasickness. Supposedly it did much good and the queen's French courtiers dubbed it *"mer malade"*— "sea sick." The more probable explanation is that the word derives from the Portuguese for quince— *marmelo*, in turn from the Latin *melimelum*, in turn from the Greek for honey (*meli*) and apple (*melon*).

The first preserve was indeed made from quince plus honey or sweet wine.

The first *orange* marmalade was made in Scotland in the eighteenth century by Janet Pierson. She already knew how to make something called "marmalet" from quince, and one day when a shipment of oranges from Spain was being sold very cheaply in the harbor, her husband, James Keiler, couldn't resist buying a large quantity. He had been so pleased with his bargain that he hadn't stopped to taste the oranges. When he got them home they turned out to be too bitter to eat. Although she'd never heard of an orange jam, Janet decided it would do no harm to experiment. So successful was she that James sold out the first batch in a few hours. He hurried back to the harbor and bought more oranges. News of the distinctive and delicious new preserve spread far and wide and it wasn't long before recipes for it began to appear in cookbooks of the period.

There are those who hold that Margaret Baxter, the wife of another Scottish grocer in Morayshire, was the true begetter. George Baxter was one of the Duke of Gordon's gardeners and it seems that the Duchess gave Margaret an old family recipe to try out, as she was noted for the jams she produced. The Duke was so impressed that he arranged for George to meet the even-then renowned Fortnum & Mason people, and soon the Baxter marmalade was finding its way all over the world.

In 1874, as the result of an Oxford don's summer visit to Scotland, marmalade was introduced to yet another grocer's wife, Mrs. Frank Cooper of Oxford, and she added her own interpretation of the recipe. Students took to it immediately, using it to make their stale bread palatable. For some reason they became fond of calling it "Squish" and it is still called by that name at Oxford breakfast parties. Traveling scholars from Oxford spread the word, and the Coopers closed their shop and went into the manufacturing business.

Also in the 1870s another couple from Paisley eliminated the extreme bitterness complained of by some admirers of Scottish marmalade. They came up with a clear, pale version full of finely shredded peel but no pith. Nowadays it's known everywhere as "golden shred" marmalade.

Spanish oranges are still the preferred fruit. The "Olde English Marmalade" made by Chivers, a descendant of the firm which began producing marmalade at Histon, Cambridge in 1877, is made primarily from Seville oranges although the firm also uses oranges grown in Malaga and Sicily. No matter where they come from, the oranges must be hand-picked to avoid any bruise to the skin—crucial because of the concentrated oils. Each orange is wrapped separately and shipped carefully packed in boxes and padded trucks. Boiling is done in small quantities to preserve the texture.

The French who care very little for any but the most rudimentary breakfast import huge quantities of marmalade. They can even be heard asking for or offering something that comes out as "du Dundi."

Cans of marmalade have been to the South Pole and the top of Everest. The preserve is regulation on British submarines. When the great *Queen Mary* still sailed the Atlantic, passengers devoured 1,600 pounds per round trip. According to Joan Hobson writing in *Gourmet* in October 1968, Sir Francis Chichester carried six pounds of it on his solo trip around the world, and no "self-respecting archaeologist goes digging in the tombs of Egypt without taking alone a crate of breakfast preserves." She reports that Princess Grace of Monaco and the King of Saudi Arabia got monthly supplies from Fortnum & Mason. Way back in 1908 Empress Alexander of Russia requested Wilkin & Sons to send her their marmalade. As did the Queen of Spain in 1912 and Queen Sophia of Greece in 1914. James Bond insists on honey with his morning toast, but Sean Connery who created the unforgettable film version of the character is often to be observed in Fortnum's buying his marmalade.

Hotels in London like the Dorchester and Claridges serve the very dark chunky version, which is fashionable. The finely shredded version is most

*Chivers'
Marmalade, the
"Aristocrat of the
Breakfast Table"—a
slogan the company
made famous during
the 1930s.*

often served on trains and planes in those somewhat off-putting little plastic containers. No room for status-husks.

Gordon Baxter, George's grandson, has introduced a "Vintage Marmalade," which is achieved by maturing the preserves in whisky casks. They are allowed to mature for five years, then reboiled and put into sealed jars. Another alcoholic marmalade is produced on the Isle of Man. Rose's Marmalade was introduced as late as 1937, but is now one of the top three sellers along with Chivers and Robertson's.

January and February find thousands of people making their own marmalade at home. Oranges are usually at their peak at that time. Here are several recipes:

Adrian Bailey in *The Cooking of the British Isles* offers this version of *Grapefruit Marmalade*: After washing and drying the grapefruit, remove skins without cutting into white pith. Cut peel into one-inch strips about one-eighth of an inch wide. Cut away and discard white outer pith. Slice fruit in half crosswise and wrap the halves, one at a time, in double thickness of damp cheesecloth. Twist, squeezing juice into bowl. Wrap and tie the pulp in the cheesecloth. Add cold water to the bowl of juice to make six pints liquid. Drop bag of pulp and strips of peel into bowl. Let stand for at least 12 hours at room temperature. Then pour contents of bowl into preserving pan and bring to boil over high heat. Reduce heat to low and simmer uncovered for two hours, stirring occasionally. Discard bag of pulp and measure the mixture. Add 1¼ pounds of sugar for each pint of mixture, stir thoroughly, and bring to boil over moderate heat. When sugar has dissolved, increase heat to high and, stirring occasionally, boil briskly for about 30 minutes until marmalade reaches a temperature of 220° F on a sugar-boiling thermometer. Remove from heat. Skim off surface foam. Ladle marmalade into hot, dry jars. Gently shake the jars as they cool to prevent peel from floating to the top.

As for the jars, an airtight seal is imperative and the covers must fit securely. To seal, use screw-on metal lids or waxed paper or cellophane held in place with rubber bands. Fill jars to within ⅛ inch from the top and store in cool, dry, dark place.

Alan Oversby's *Grapefruit Marmalade* (about 9 pounds):

6 lbs sugar
4 medium-size grapefruits
3 lemons
2 Seville oranges (used because they have many pips—not so much for flavor—grapefruit seem to have no pips these days and you need them for pectin)

Slice the peel fairly thickly [here Mr. Oversby differs from Mr. Bailey], removing some of the white pith if it is too thick. Cut fruit in half. Squeeze out the juice and pips. Tie pips and any excess pith in a piece of muslin. It's best to let the sliced peel and bag

There's nothing quite like an Olde English breakfast. **CHIVERS**

One of the distinctive contemporary ads introduced by Chivers in which an orange takes the form of the product.

> "She looked at the sides and noticed that they were filled with cupboards and shelves . . . She took down a jar from one of the shelves as she passed; it was labelled 'Orange Marmalade' but to her great disappointment it was empty; she did not like to drop the jar for fear of killing someone underneath . . . so managed to put it in one of the cupboards as she fell past it."
>
> *Alice in Wonderland*

of pips and pith soak overnight in a bowl with two pints of water along with the squeezed-out juice.

Put peel, still in the same water, and bag of pips, in a preserving pan along with four more pints of cold water. Bring to a boil, then simmer for two hours. Remove the bag of pips and pith, squeezing it *well*. Add the sugar and dissolve over gentle heat, stirring all the time. Bring to boil until setting point is reached—220°F—on a cooking thermometer. Remove any scum that has formed and let the marmalade cool for about 15 to 20 minutes (for evenly distributed peel, stir gently); pour into clean, warm jars. Cover, seal, label, store in cool place. (Mr. Oversby suggests sealing with paraffin wax—so much nicer than paper—which can be washed and re-used.)

Mr. Oversby started making his own marmalade as the result of his having been given a beautiful brass preserving pan that had belonged to his great grandmother. His sister used to give him "the odd jar" of marmalade *she* had made and it so delighted him that he felt his beautiful pan should be used for more than ornamentation. "As soon as I saw my first glowing, shining pot full of gold, I knew I was hooked—a large, golden-brass pan filled with yellow and orange peel floating in water: total beauty: and the smell as it simmered on the stove! Even the jars standing in rows on the shelf when they are stored—that too has its beauty and gives a feeling of satisfaction.

"I am almost obsessed with the necessity of making more marmalade every new January and February and am no so far in advance that we are eating marmalade made three years ago—and the taste really does improve as it matures."

Patricia Holden White's *Orange and Apricot Marmalade* from *Food as Presents* (yield: about 6 lbs; keeps very well):

2 lbs oranges
1 large lemon
6 oz dried apricots, washed and finely chopped
2 pints water
4 lbs preserving sugar

Scrub oranges and lemon, cut into quarters (reserving pips) and chop coarsely. Tie pips in a piece of clean cloth. Put all fruit and pips in a preserving pan, cover with water and leave overnight to soak. Bring fruit to the boil gently, uncovered, for $1\frac{1}{2}$ hours, by which time the peel should be tender. The cooking time required will depend on the kind of oranges you use, so keep an eye on the pan. When the peel is tender, remove the bag of pips and take the pan from the heat. Add sugar, stirring constantly without boiling, until it is completely dissolved. Bring marmalade to the boil for about 20 minutes stirring only to keep the peel from sticking. Test for set. (If you don't have a sugar thermometer, testing for set can also be done by dropping a bit of jam or jelly on a cold plate and allowing it to cool—be sure to remove preserving pan from heat as well, to avoid overcooking. When the blob of cooled jam wrinkles at the push of your finger, a set has been obtained.) Allow to rest for 20 minutes before potting.

The fabled Mrs. Beeton sensibly reminds us that in marmalade making, otherwise essentially the same as jam making, the citron peel takes longer to soften and that the pips and pith are important ingredients because of their pectin [cheers for Mr. Oversby] and should not be discarded. She suggests tying the muslin bag containing the latter to the handle of the pan to aid in removing it when adding the sugar. Other tips: as an aid to peeling, soak the fruit in boiling water for one to two minutes before drying and peeling; be sure to cut peel into small shreds as it will swell during cooking.

Dorothy Hartley in her *Food in England* gives a very old and delicious recipe for *Quince Marmalade*:

Collect your quinces, and pare and chop up at least half of them (including the least ripe), just cover with water, and set to boil to pulp. When soft, rub all through a sieve. To this golden red thickness now add the remaining of the quinces, pared, cored and cut into neat sections. Set the pan back to simmer gently and steadily, till the whole quinces are almost soft, and the pulp pretty thick (stir well, or it will burn). Now add sugar, 3 lbs to a quart of the pulp. When the sugar has dissolved, boil fast till it sets when tried. It should be very firm, and a dark bright-red color. Slices cut from it make good garnishes for plain white "creams" or it can be melted and used as a sauce over blancmanges.

Grandmother Brown's *Rhubarb Marmalade* from Dale Brown's *American Cooking*:

Combine 2 lbs rhubarb coarsely chopped with 3 tablespoons orange juice and equal amount of lemon juice in enameled pan. Bring to boil, cover, reduce the heat and simmer for about an hour, or until rhubarb is soft. Stir in 2 lbs sugar and, stirring constantly, boil rapidly for about 5 minutes, or until mixture is translucent and lightly holds its shape in a spoon. Turn off the heat, stir in 2 oranges, peeled, seeded, sectioned, and one lemon, the same. Add grated rind of 1 orange and 1 lemon and $\frac{1}{2}$ lb halved walnuts. Still stirring occasionally, let the marmalade cool to room temperature, then pour it into sterilized glasses and seal with paraffin wax.

On a Midwestern Farm

In a delightful book of reminiscences, THE COUNTRY KITCHEN, *written by Della Lutes and published in the 1930s, we are given a very clear picture of a Midwestern farm breakfast.*

My father came to the breaking of his night's fast after a preliminary hour's wrestling with chores, and he went from the table to a day's work in which fields had to be ploughed, seed sown, hay cut, grain reaped, corn husked. To men like him, breakfast meant meat and potatoes—the chief staples around which the meal revolved. And meat usually meant pork, in one form or another, commonly salted. . . . In the butchering season there was fresh pork, and liver; later on there would be sausages, or smoked ham and shoulder; in the early spring and summer, eggs. After a rainy day, when the men had not been able to work in the fields, there might be fish. But always there were potatoes. Sometimes they were boiled, with an accompaniment of milk gravy or creamed codfish; again they were sliced and crisply fried; or they might be baked, with pink slices of home-cured ham and gravy.

Our home-cured ham was like nothing I have seen or tasted since. The difference between commercially smoked hams and those cured in the little slant-roofed brick shanty out behind our house is traceable, I suspect, to the fact that the former are not smoked with corncobs. Some of the commercial houses burn hickory sticks, yes, but no corncobs. If you have ever smelled freshly shucked corncobs

burning, you can imagine what that did to a ham.

When it came to cooking the ham for breakfast, my mother sliced it about one-fourth of an inch thick and freshened it in cold water brought to warm on the back of the stove. It was then drained and wiped dry. In its own firm border of fat it was fried slowly to sweet perfection, and then removed to a hot platter. The remaining fat was allowed to reach a smoking heat . . . and into this my mother sifted flour to a bubbling paste, stirring while it seethed and browned. When enough flour was added to absorb the fat, warmed milk was stirred in gradually and evenly to make a gravy having the consistency of heavy cream. It was then salted and peppered to taste.

Our breakfasts did not begin with fruit or fruit juices. If we had fruit at all, it was eaten with fried-cakes and cookies; but in general fruit was reserved for supper. . . .

My father liked eggs for breakfast—two or three, at least—and he wanted them fried or boiled. If boiled, they must be boiled hard. But a hard *fried* egg was his abomination.

Few women can fry an egg as my mother could. Her technique was perfect, and the result was no leathery mass of frizzled white and broken yolk, but an intact globule of filmed yellow set in a circle of congealed albumen. She fried eggs in the fat from bacon or ham, whichever happened to be in use. This fat was made hot—sizzling but never smoking; if it was too hot, it was drawn to the back of the stove until there was no danger of browning the thin edge of the white before the yolk was cooked.

Each egg (taken from the nest the night before) was broken separately and gently into the sizzling fat, and never were so many introduced into the spider at one time that their edges mingled. Then my mother stood by, spooning the hot fat over them until the yolks presented an opaque appearance and the whites were coagulated but not hardened. They were then, at the exact moment of perfection, taken from the spider with a pancake turner and laid on a warm platter along with the ham, rosily tender and faintly browned, or bacon, done to a curl but never to a crisp. An egg fried in this fashion, its qualities and virtues instantly sealed within it by a hot, sweet coating of honest fat, cannot be too great a tax on the digestive machinery. Numberless were the fried eggs my father consumed, and he bore up under them until well past his eighty-fifth birthday.

A poached egg is another dish apparently difficult to achieve, but it was not beyond the scope of my mother's culinary art. The water, she maintained, should be at the hard-boiling point when the eggs are slid into it, one at a time, and after that it must be allowed only to bubble. This is accomplished by drawing the pan to one side of the stove, while the bubbling water is spooned over the eggs until the yolks are filmed and the whites "set."

For the more inexperienced . . . a teaspoonful of vinegar will help to keep the white of the egg in shape and does not affect the flavor. But it is care and attention that bring the perfect result.

"You have to stand over things," my mother said, "to make 'em right." . . .

Salt mackerel was one of my father's favorite dishes. It came in a "kit" or small wooden pail and smelled to heaven when it was opened. For breakfast a fish was washed, scraped on the inside, put in cold water the night before, and set on the back of the stove (in which there would be no fire) to freshen. In the morning the water was changed and the frying pan ("spider," we called it) brought forward to heat slowly. When everything else was ready to serve, the water was drained off . . . and the fish allowed to pan-broil for about ten minutes. . . .

Fried mush came along in the fall, after the first harvest of winter corn and before the pancake season set in, and again in the spring when the batter pitcher was washed and put away. Fried mush for breakfast followed a preceding supper of mush and milk. My mother made her mush by sifting yellow corn meal, fresh from the mill, into an iron kettle of boiling salted water; with one hand she sifted the meal while with the other she stirred it with a wooden spoon. It was then drawn to the back of the stove to bubble and sputter and spurt for an hour or longer—and woe to you if it happened to spurt onto bare hand or arm while stirring.

Whatever mush was left over after supper was packed into a greased bread tin. In the morning this was sliced and fried in hot fat, and eaten with butter and syrup.

We did not have maple syrup. There were a few maple trees on our place and my father would occasionally tap them to get enough sap for a drink; or, as a special treat, my mother would sometimes boil down a little sap into sugar. Although other farms about us boasted a "bush," and maple syrup was not an unknown luxury in southern Michigan, it was not common as it is now. Instead, we had sugar syrup—white and brown sugar boiled together in a small amount of water—and it answered the purpose very well. And, of course, the covered glass dish of honey—honey in the comb and fresh from the hive—was as customary an accessory to the breakfast table as the butter dish.

Frequently there were hot breads. Usually sourmilk biscuits, since there were always sour milk and sour cream on hand. Both of these are a considerable luxury, but in my humble opinion no baking-powder biscuit yet devised can compare with the "sour milk and sody" kind. . . .

For Sunday-morning breakfast (because they require longer cooking) nothing could be better than popovers . . . (but I never saw one in my mother's house!). . . . Then there was johnnycake, but for this you *must* have buttermilk. . . . Fried cakes [dough-nuts] were always, month in and month out, as much a part of the first meal of the day as coffee. I think my father would have considered it a personal affront to ask him to make a breakfast without fried cakes. He did not "dunk" them, and he did not hold with men who dunked them. I remember his once reproving a hired man who had the habit. "Well, Curt," he said, "see you been hobnobbin' with the Lunkers." (The Lunkers were a family that lived down on the crossroads and were known for their slovenly habits.) I felt a little sorry for the man, who laughed awkwardly and soon after left the table. . . .

In winter, breakfast took on a new meaning, for then the fried mush, johnnycake, or ordinary plain bread gave way to buckwheat cakes. There were differences in taste regarding the lacing of these cakes. Some insisted that the only proper sauce was butter; others preferred sugar and thick cream; still others liked to pour over their cakes the hot brown fat from fried ham or pork. But the general preference was for butter and syrup. . . .

After the buckwheat crop was harvested, my father, never a patient man, could hardly wait for the pancake season to open. My mother did not like to begin too early, for, like other habits, once started it was difficult to break, and the routine lasted until spring, without respite. This meant added details in an already crowded day of petty tasks: the cakes had to be "set" the night before, and while the rest of us were at breakfast she had to stand over a hot fire to cook them, for she would not compromise with her belief that buckwheat cakes should be eaten direct from the griddle, a theory in which my father upheld her to the teeth. Ours was not a large family, but there was often a hired man, frequently a visiting relative, sometimes the itinerant preacher, a seamstress, or perhaps the ragman spending the night. And my father himself was no light eater. So, if my mother seemed to dally about beginning the ritual, she had good cause. . . .

Sausage was a frequent accompaniment of buckwheat cakes. Its odor and flavor still haunt me, proof that some mysterious ingredient in its making has been lost to mankind. As I pondered this culinary conundrum, the answer suddenly came to me. It was the *sage*. The whole secret lay in the sage. We grew our own in a neat little row along the garden's edge, picked and dried it, and crumbled it—aromatic, fresh, and pungent—into the meat. But, on second thought, perhaps the pepper may have had something to do with it, too. For my mother ground her own pepper in a little wooden mill that she held in her hand or on her lap. . . .

What did children eat at those breakfasts of meat and potatoes and pancakes? Why, we ate meat and potatoes and pancakes. We drank quantities of milk, ate acres of bread, consumed butter by the pound, and we also ate doughnuts and cookies by the dozen.

WALKER ART GALLERY, LIVERPOOL

My pleasantest memory is of breakfast in a nice warm kitchen on a cold morning, with my little glass mug of milk (it had "A Good Girl" printed on it in gold), a huge slice of bread all buttered at once (there was not a single book of etiquette in our community), some little pancakes just for me, and my eye on the cookie plate. . . .

If to eat a hearty breakfast meant getting up at six o'clock, or even before, we got up, and ate with the family, and went out sustained by both good cheer and good food. . . .

An English farm breakfast similar in scene to that eaten on a farm in the American Midwest. A painting by F. G. Cotman.

119

At the Ritz

The Ritz? Well, yes. Because, obviously, there are a number of superb hotels in the world, a number of them legendary—like Raffles in Singapore or Shepheard's in Cairo—but there is only *one* hotel which has given an adjective to the language, an image of the superior, the unique, and that is the Hotel Ritz in Paris. F. Scott Fitzgerald, looking for a title that would instantly call to mind the superlative, came up with "The Diamond as Big as the Ritz" and the reader saw immediately that he wasn't dealing just with size. But the adjective I'm talking about is *ritzy*. We say, "It's a very ritzy place." Or some of us do. Then there's the expression "putting on the Ritz."

There are now eight Ritz hotels in the world—in London, Paris, Madrid, Barcelona, Lisbon, Montreal, Boston and Chicago. If you are surprised not to read "New York" as well, you have reason. There was a New York Ritz once. It had a wonderful oval restaurant and a kitchen on every floor, but it went the way of so many things in New York, the Restless City. More cheeringly, the one in Chicago is brand new, having only opened in December 1975. All of these hotels are in their separate ways superior establishments, but there really is only one *real* Ritz and that's the original one—in Paris.

Founded in 1898 by César Ritz, it still dominates the mythology of hotels. It is situated in the beautiful Place Vendôme and has no enormous electric sign or bold marquee to identify it. I suppose you could miss it if you didn't know it was there. The Vendôme entrance opens into the reception and writing rooms, to carpeted corridors and a lovely garden restaurant, and eventually, a street away, to the bars on the Rue Cambon. The worlds of fame, of wealth, of power have all experienced the Ritz. They still do. But times have changed. The chefs have lightened the heavy, rich foods of the old days with an intelligent assent to modern ideas about diet and health. And they have done so without any loss in quality. Service is still exceptional (guests can order an omelette, sole, steak, etc. from 10 P.M. till midnight, and after midnight such things as consommé, a chicken sandwich or a Continental Breakfast).

Breakfast, in your room or perhaps in one of the restaurants or the garden, reflects the great changes that have been wrought in the world. No mention of champagne or caviar. Just: coffee, "infusion," "American coffee," tea, chocolate; eggs—poached, hard-boiled, baked, boiled; omelette—plain, cheese, ham; eggs and bacon; grilled ham, cold ham, bacon; cornflakes, porridge, oatmeal; cheeses; yogurt; fruit compote; oranges; macedoine of fruits; fresh grapefruit, tomato, lemon, and orange juice. That's all. I confess to a certain disappointment, although I dare say that if a guest wanted something a bit more imaginative, he or she could get it simply by ordering it in advance.

Breakfast at the handsome Ritz in Madrid just

across from the Prado, starts out promisingly with a dramatic menu cover showing a single red rose touched with dew. However, the offerings inside are no more exciting than those in Paris: coffee, tea, chocolate; *croissant*, *brioche*, marmalade, butter (none of these are listed in the Paris menu; I suppose the French take breads and accompaniments for granted); the standard juices; fruit; the standard egg dishes; cold ham; yogurt; cheeses; porridge; cornflakes. The Continental Breakfast listed for room service names Nescafé along with the other beverages. And Swiss rolls are offered. But the rest is basically the same as that listed for the dining rooms. I suppose these foods are what the majority of travelers want—even the rich ones. I just wonder if that was true when the Duke of Windsor occupied his favorite suite on the fifth floor or the Maharajah of Kapantala was married there in the twenties.

The London Ritz, which has been going through difficult times lately but is still an enchanting place in which to take tea or a meal, has recently been bought by an investment group who promise elaborate renovations without changing the beautiful dining rooms or the Winter Garden. Susan Campbell and Alexandra Towle in their delightful *Cheap Eats in London* quite rightly include the Ritz. They note that breakfast (which is not high-priced) is served from 7 to 10 A.M. in "A beautiful oval room . . . with a richly gilded ceiling . . .; comfortable sofas and upholstered chairs, some pale green, some rose pink . . . group around little tables covered with crisp white damask cloths . . . curtains of rose brocade swagged around the beautifully proportioned windows . . . the soothing sound of running water from the magnificent fountain framed by an ornate alcove."

And the food? A bit more varied than those described so far. Perhaps being English has something to do with it. Anyway, aside from the usual beverages, breads, cereals and egg dishes, there are fried or grilled sole, kippers, grilled tomatoes and mushrooms and sausages. Still, not all *that* adventurous in the land of kedgeree, kidneys and Finnan Haddie.

I got no response to my inquiries from the Lisbon or Barcelona Ritzes, but I imagine the one in Lisbon, which is owned by the same group as the one in Madrid, offers substantially the same breakfast. And I suspect pretty much the same thing of the Ritz in Barcelona. Which has, by the way, one of the most remarkable eating areas in the world (or did when I stayed there in 1958—Continental Breakfast of *café au lait* and *croissants*)—an outdoor "room," "roofed" over by a single enormous wisteria vine trained over a trellis, its huge, twisted trunk like a work of sculpture, rising at one end of the space next to a fountain in which fruit float to keep cool.

The Montreal Ritz serves breakfasts similar to those of the Boston and Chicago versions (see below) with a few nice variations such as Apple Sauce, Dore

Meunière, Broiled Canadian Bacon and Windsor Bacon. Besides the *à la carte* menu the hotel offers four grades of breakfast in ascending order of cost: The Empress (toast and rolls; beverage); The Continental (juice, fruit or cereal; toast and rolls; beverage); The Canadian (same with the addition of one egg with ham, bacon or sausage); The Club (both juice, fruit and cereal and two eggs or pancakes both with ham, etc.).

The Boston Ritz is actually called the Ritz-Carlton (none of these hotels, by the way, have anything to do with the Paris Ritz except for their name which they got permission to use from César Ritz or his family). Here, rather charmingly, the menu is much more varied. Beyond the usual, we can choose a baked apple with cream; stewed prunes; Kadota figs in syrup; cold cereals served with sliced banana; wheat or buckwheat cakes; French toast served with pure maple syrup or honey; a 5-ounce breakfast steak; Finnan Haddie in cream (London please note!); broiled Boston scrod; hashed brown, hashed in cream or French fried potatoes; blueberry or corn muffins; Danish pastries; cinnamon rolls; raisin toast; English muffins; hot chocolate with cream; Sanka; Instant Postum.

Perhaps because it is so new, the Chicago Ritz-Carlton tries even harder. Set next to the spectacular John Hancock building at the glamorous Water Tower area of North Michigan Avenue, it doesn't really "begin" until you enter the lobby on the twelfth floor of the condominium building it shares. Each floor has its own pantry for room service at any hour. The breakfast menu, while basically the same as that for Boston, does offer some nice additions—strawberries as well as bananas with cold cereals; waffles; smoked salmon omelettes; roast beef hash; center-cut pork chops; lamb chops (what's happened to the famous English mixed grill?); chicken hash in cream (which would have pleased the Duke of Windsor—see "Some People . . ."); calf's liver sautéed; buttermilk and nonfat milk.

Still, I'm surprised that neither of the American hotels offers yogurt, or bagels for that matter, and that *none* of them list smoked salmon or caviar.

At Breakfast

Not quite
spherical
White
Oddly closed
and without a lid

A smooth miracle
here in my hand
Has it slid
from my sleeve?

The shape
of this box
keels me oval
Heels feel
its bottom
Nape knocks
its top

Seated
like a foetus
I look for
the dream-seam

What's inside?
A sun?
Off with its head
though it hasn't any
or is all head no body
a
One

Neatly
the knife scalps it
I scoop out
the braincap
soft
sweetly shuddering

Mooncream
this could be
Spoon
laps the larger
crescent
loosens a gilded
nucleus
from warm pap
a lyrical food

Opened
a seamless miracle
Ate a sun-germ
Good

May Swenson

English Breakfast...

The Big Breakfast? The Saxons breakfasted on ale, cold pork and coarse dark bread. In the Middle Ages the rich ate bread, boiled beef, mutton, salt herring, wine and ale—not *too* huge. The poor, of whom there were a good deal more, subsisted on bread, salt pork or bacon when they could get it, fish on Fridays, and ale. This diet continued for about five hundred years. Charles Cooper in *The English Table in History and Literature* reports that the first Elizabeth "breakfasted upon solid principles and materials" along with her maids. "Beef and beer were consumed at breakfast—'a repast for a plough-man!' it may be said. . . ." Well, maybe, but not much compared to an honest Victorian country meal.

Up to the end of the eighteenth century, breakfast was mainly thought of as a masculine meal. The gentry in fact breakfasted separately: the husband ate cold meats, pies, ale and claret; the wife ate cake and drank tea and chocolate at ten. Farmers of the period up early to work the fields ate bread and ale.

An eighteenth-century parson in East Anglia recorded in his diary that on October 7, 1794, he had breakfasted on "Chocolate, green and brown tea, hot rolls, dried toast, bread and butter, honey, tongue and ham grated very small." Very modest fare.

In 1820 Washington Irving in his *Sketch Book* wrote of a breakfast of what a "Squire denominated true old English fare. He indulged in some bitter lamentations over modern breakfasts of tea and toast, which he censured as among the causes of modern effeminacy and weak nerves, and the decline of the old English heartiness. . . ." Irving noted that at the Squire's "there was a brave display of cold meats, wine, and ale on the sideboard."

A hundred years earlier Martin wrote in his *Description of the Western Isles*, that "Brochan, i.e. oatmeal boiled with water with some bread, is the constant food of several thousands of both sexes in this and other islands during winter and spring, yet they go under many fatigues by sea and land, and are very healthful." Brochan is, of course, porridge, and, along with marmalade, one of the standard dishes given to the world by Scotland.

Even earlier, in 1597, Monipennie, traveling in the Highlands, observed that the people "make their bread of oates and barly (which are the onely kinds of grayne that grow in these parts). . . . They take a little of it in the morning, and so, passing to . . . any other business, content themselves therewith . . . till even. They made only two meals in the day—the

Then and Now

little meal about noon, and the *great* meal towards evening."

Maybe it depends on who and where you are. Another account, dated 1708, has it that in Scotland "No people eat better, or have greater varieties of flesh, fish, wild and tame fowl, than the Scots nobility and gentry in their own country, where they can furnish their tables with ten dishes cheaper than the English can provide three of the same kinds. . . . The tradesmen, farmers, and common people are not excessive devourers of flesh, as men of the same rank are in England. Milkmeats and oatmeal, several ways prepared, and kale and roots dressed in several manners, is the constant diet of the poor people (for roast-meat is seldom had but on gaudy-days); and with this kind of food they enjoy a better state of health than their southern neighbours, who fare higher."

According to F. Marian McNeill (*The Book of Breakfasts*), the Normans superimposed themselves over the Saxons and "feudalized" the English kitchen much more so than in Scotland, Wales or Ireland. Scott described this feudal breakfast in *Old Mortality*: "The breakfast of Lady Margaret Bellenden no more resembled a modern *déjeuner*, than the great stone hall at Tillietudlem could brook comparison with a modern drawing-room. No tea, no coffee, no variety of rolls, but solid and substantial viands—the priestly ham, the knightly sirloin, the noble baron of beef, the princely venison pasty; while silver flagons, saved with difficulty from the claws of the Covenanters, now mantled, some with ale, some with mead, and some with generous wines of various qualities and descriptions."

In the middle of the seventeenth century, as noted by G. M. Trevelyan, breakfast in most upper and middle-class homes consisted of no more than a "morning draft" of ale with a little bread and butter.

The introduction of coffee, probably during Cromwell's Protectorate, and tea, in England in 1666 by Lord Arlington, and in Scotland in 1681 by Mary of Modena, wife of James VII, began the change of everything. More and more it replaced beer, wine and ale. In 1729 Macintosh of Borlum sadly complained that on visiting a friend's house "of a morning I used to be asked if I had my morning draught yet. I am now asked if I have had my tea. And in lieu of . . . strong ale and toast, and after a dram of good wholesome Scots spirits, there is now the tea-kettle put to the fire, the tea-table and silver and china equipage brought in, and marmalade and cream."

But to continue the seesaw of lots and little a bit longer, Humphrey Lyttleton remembers as a child staying at some stately home or other where "the Edwardian style still prevailed. Innumerable silver dishes were lined up on a hot plate, offering a staggering choice as one moved along them raising the lids. Eggs boiled, scrambled or fried, bacon, ham, kidney, huge flapping field mushrooms, sausages, kippers, haddock, sometimes even a cheese soufflé, and kedgeree." Many people attribute this last dish to Scotland for some reason, but it is Indian in origin and a result of the British Raj.

What we think of as the "classic" British Breakfast only really developed in the eighteenth century when it became a time-taking family affair and as such flourished during the Victorian and Edwardian period right up to World War I. There was time and there were plenty of servants. This was only true for the privileged, of course. The rest of the people went down the scale to the workhouses with their stale bread and watery porridge. Farmers fared better as they usual do, having access to most of the raw materials of a decent breakfast.

Harold Wilshaw wrote of pre-war breakfast at The Red Lion in Salisbury (*Guardian*, October 30, 1975): "While it had become outdated even in the thirties, the standard breakfast there, after you had nodded at or ignored the cereals, porridge and so on, always consisted of a grilled sole, or poached haddock or kipper, followed by eggs, bacon, sausage and kidneys, or a chop or piece of steak. Hot rolls, toast and marmalade were there for the hungry, while a solicitous wine waiter went round taking orders for beer, which came in silver pots."

To be honest, you take your chances searching for the Big English Breakfast these days. It does exist. I've had it in the country. I've had it, or part of it, in a train. An extremely apropos letter from a Mr. J. L. Nichols of Uckfield, Sussex, recently appeared in the letters column of the *Caterer*, a trade publication. He is commenting on a picture in a previous issue showing a Continental breakfast and captioned "What more do you need?" I quote in part: "If the question is directed to me personally the answer is 'nothing,' but if to overseas tourists and many English holidaymakers it is 'a full English breakfast.' It is not generally appreciated by hoteliers that the traditional English breakfast is famed worldwide and is a major tourist attraction. . . .

"One can equate a foreign tourist who cannot obtain an English breakfast in his hotel with a disappointed tourist. To meet this important demand hoteliers have three options: (1) to quote for bed and English breakfast; (2) to quote for bed and Continental breakfast with English breakfast as an optional extra; (3) to quote for bed only with both English and Continental breakfasts as extras. . . .

"Any hotelier with a foreign clientele will certainly offer a good English breakfast some way or another, if he needs return business and recommendations. And who doesn't?"

In a hurry or not, the experience of a really well prepared and served "English Breakfast" is one of the "newest and nicest" experiences a foreigner can have in England and is worth slowing down for. Where it is gone or going let's hope for its revival. Where it continues, long may it live!

"Bangers and mash," tea and marmalade, watched over by Her Majesty the Queen in this satiric painting by Malcolm Fowler.

Coffee

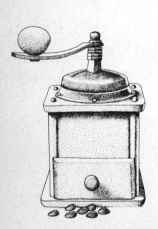

There must be, if not as many *kinds* of coffee, at least as many ways of brewing it as there are humans. There's percolator coffee and drip coffee and *filtre* coffee and *espresso* coffee and instant coffee and freeze-dried coffee. There's vacuum-made coffee and automatic coffee that starts bubbling as soon as the alarm-radio sends out its plastic cheer. There's coffee you force through a kind of plunger-strainer. There's coffee you throw into a pan along with an egg shell. There's coffee cooked under high pressure. Coffee ground for each cup. Coffee eased through special paper. Coffee poured in duet with hot (not boiling) milk. Coffee heated electrically, by gas, by sterno, on an open fire.

There's coffee for one, for two, for a hundred; black coffee, white coffee; weak coffee, strong coffee; sweet coffee, bitter coffee; spiked coffee; Brazilian and African; island and mainland; airport and turnpike; railroad and drugstore. There's café coffee, hotel coffee, motel coffee. There's coffee on shipboard, yachtboard, and cruiser. There's coffee in airplanes and subways and trucks; in bathrooms; at poolside; in submarines. For all I know there's coffee in phone booths and belfries.

It has been described as viscous, as wishy-washy, as tepid or scalding, dreary or gourmet, aroma-filled or flat. As bad coffee. As good coffee. As rich coffee. As poor coffee. Fresh. Stale. There is caffeine-free coffee and, now, coffee-bags.

There are tribal events known as "coffee breaks" and "coffee claches." There are people called "coffee hounds," "coffee freaks," or simply "coffee addicts." Théophile Gautier wrote of his friend Balzac, who was definitely one of the latter: "[His] coffee was composed of three different kinds of bean. Bourbon, Martinique and Mocha. He bought the Bourbon in the Rue de Montblanc, the Martinique in the Rue des Vielles and the Mocha in the Faubourg St. Germain . . . I repeatedly accompanied Balzac on his shopping expeditions. Each time it involved half a day's journey right across Paris. But to Balzac good coffee was worth the trouble."

Balzac would have been right at home at super-specialty shops like Freed, Teller & Freed, which dates back to pre-earthquake San Francisco and offers twenty-five varieties of coffee, or H.R. Higgins Ltd. in London with their wonderful unblended coffees from such places as Costa Rica, Colombia, Brazil, Ethiopia, Java, and their exceptional Chagga coffees grown by Tanzanian tribesmen. A typical list of superior-quality coffees (which can be ordered by mail) is put out by another distinguished London merchant, Whittard & Co., Ltd. They list their coffees in descending order of strength. The coffees range from dark pure beans such as Santo and Java, which are listed as *High Roast Continental*; through *Strong Coffee, Medium Roast*, which includes blends like East African and Central American, Colombia, Mocha and Mysore; to *Medium Coffee, Medium Roast* blends of African and Central American, Costa Rican, Kenyan, Caribbean Mountain and Brazilian. A Coffee and Chicory Mix is described as "very strong, piquant, economical."

Soyer in *Pantropheon* (1853) relates various theories about the famous brew: that drinking coffee was introduced by a prior who noted the effect the plant produced on goats and tried it out on his monks to keep them awake during divine service; that a mufti, wanting to surpass the most religious dervishes in devotion, used it to banish sleep. Nowadays, it "may almost be classed among the articles of greatest necessity." Soyer adds sensibly, "It would be useless here to describe the different methods of making coffee . . ."

Because of its expense people have long been trying to create substitutes—roasted acorns in Switzerland; roasted rye in the mountains of Virginia; coffee mixed with chicory in Belgium, a practice still widely used in Europe to this day. In Flanders, lupin was cultivated. Gypsies and herbalists make coffee from dandelion roots which they dry and grind—reportedly good for the liver and good with milk.

Beauvais speaks of coffee as strength-giving when drunk pure—"It is doubtless for [this reason] that the inhabitants of the colonies take it three and four times a day—that is, at four o'clock in the morning, a very strong infusion, sometimes without sugar; at breakfast, with milk. . . ." Of the date of coffee's exact introduction into Europe not much is known. Mention of it is made in 1583. Prospero Alpini described coffee in Egypt in about 1591. In 1614 Bacon wrote of it. And in 1621, Meissner published a treatise on it. Not until 1645 was it drunk in Italy. The first London coffee houses opened in 1652 and the Paris cafés in 1669—at which time coffee was said to cost forty crowns a pound! The fashion for coffee in Paris was largely the doing of Soliman Ago who was the ambassador from Turkey at that time. Sweden got it in 1674 where it was used medically. Supposedly the first person to drink it with milk was Nierehoff, the Dutch ambassador to China.

Of coffee's physical effects, Virey, a nineteenth-century French doctor and politician, wrote: "It accelerates the circulation of the blood, but sometimes causes palpitation of the heart and giddiness; it has been thought to occasion apoplexy and paralysis. Nevertheless, celebrated writers—such as Fontenelle and Voltaire—made constant use of it, almost to an abuse. They were told, *it is a slow poison*; it was indeed slow for these learned men, who died, the one at a hundred, the other eighty-four years of age. However, at the present time coffee is a beverage whose power over our intellectual or moral habits has, perhaps, never been calculated as it deserves, since it has become general, and almost suppressed the drunkenness which disgraced our ancestors. . . ."

Mme. de Sevigne predicted at a moralistic moment, *"Le café et Racine passeront."* That was a couple of hundred years ago and she was wrong on both counts.

To the Bedouin of Jordan, coffee is used as a social tool and its preparation and serving involves a special ritual. According to Shelagh Weir of the British Museum Department of Ethnography, "tea and coffee are usually prepared by the host himself. Upon the arrival of a visitor, tea is brewed up in a kettle and poured into a small glass with sugar, then, if coffee is not already simmering in a pot on the fire, fresh coffee will be made. . . . Dried camel dung and small bushes, such as the fragrant wormwood (*shīh*), which will grow all over south Jordan, are used as fuel. The beans are taken from their container . . . and placed in an iron ladle (*miḥmāṣeh*) over the fire. As the beans roast they are stirred with a rod (*yad*) to prevent them burning. They are then turned out into a wooden cooling dish (*mabradah*) which is usually oval or rectangular in shape. . . . When the beans have cooled they are poured from the dish, which usually has a spout for this purpose, into a mortar. . . . The host pounds the beans with the pestle in a rhythmic beat which can be heard for some distance and advertises the presence of guests to the rest of the encampment. Meanwhile the largest of three or four coffee pots has been filled with water and placed on the fire. When the water boils, the ground coffee is tossed in, and the pot is returned to the fire and allowed to rise to the boil several times. Then a few cardamon seeds (*hayl*) are pounded in the mortar and put in another smaller pot, and the coffee is poured over them and allowed to simmer. It is then strained into a third smaller pot from which it is poured into the cups. Some coffee pots have a lid on the spout, or sticks are stuffed down it, to prevent the grounds and seeds escaping. Coffee is always poured with the pot in the left hand and the cup or cups in the right. The cups (*finjān* or *finjāl*) used by the Bedouin are very small and have no handles. Only a little coffee is poured into each cup, and each guest is offered three helpings after which it is polite to indicate that one has had sufficient by shaking the cup when handing it back to the host."

It is interesting to compare this elaborately ordered ritual with the informal directions for making coffee given by Mrs. Beeton. (She is not, of course, dealing with an occasion involving guests.) Speaking with her usual simplicity and straightforwardness she feels that the best coffee is made from beans just roasted and ground. Ideally, only as many beans as are needed should be ground. Beans should be stored in an airtight container. There are a number of ways to make coffee: warm a china jug, put in coarsely ground coffee (about two dessert-spoons per person), pour in boiling water, stir vigorously. Allow to stand 1 minute. Skim off floating grounds. Let stand another 4 minutes, closely covered. Pour slowly or strain into second china jug and serve. Another method is to put coarsely ground coffee with water in an enameled saucepan and bring almost to a boil. Lower heat and simmer for 3 minutes. Dash in one teaspoon of cold water to settle grounds. Strain into warm coffee pot. Or you can use a percolator—over fire, or electric. (The thing to watch for here is that the coffee isn't allowed to continue recirculating after it is properly brewed.) Normal time, gently percolating, about 6 to 8 minutes.

"Irish Coffee" is great for brunch (as well as after dinner), and is made with Irish whiskey, coffee and whipped cream.

Coffee pot of brass made in Syria and used by the Bedouin and townspeople of the Levant.
THE BRITISH MUSEUM

"Coffee glides down into one's stomach and sets everything in motion. One's ideas advance in columns en route like battalions of the *grande armée*. Memories come up at the double bearing the standards which are to lead the troops into battle ... the artillery of logic thunders along with its supply wagons and shells. Brilliant notions join in the combat as sharpshooters. . . ."

Balzac

131

Memorable Mornings

> Complacencies of the peignoir, and late
> Coffee and oranges in a sunny chair.
> *from* "SUNDAY MORNING" *by Wallace Stevens*

We've all had them. Have them. Among mine: at a superb old chateau called Viescamp in the mysterious French Dordogne region, in the warm big kitchen, the others not down yet, a huge cup of *café au lait*, fresh country bread and home-made jam; Georgette, the cook who looks like a lady painted by Boucher—pale silver and rose—preparing my eggs and getting organized for lunch. Strong coffee, hot milk, *brioches* and squares of marvelous bitter chocolate at a roadside café in Holland. A *pensione* in Forio d'Ischia, an island in the Bay of Naples where I lived one summer—coffee and milk, fresh fruit, local grapes usually, still-warm bread, honey and marmalade, my room smelling of lemons from the grove outside my window and of flowers from the bouquet arranged for me by the maid. City apartments in Brussels and Copenhagen, New York and San Francisco. A substantial "farmer's breakfast" (eggs, potatoes, onions, peppers, sausage all cooked together) in a country village in Bavaria on tour, with friends, of the confectionary-like Rococco churches. In a country house near Grasse in the south of France, beneath grape leaves, curious bees investigating the honey

and jam. On a high terrace in Capri lit by glowing geraniums and bougainvillaea. On farms. On trains. On ships. On planes. Often in the comforting warmth of the Café Deux Maggots in Paris with the serene Simone de Beauvoir working away at a nearby table, undisturbed by the blasé waiters and respectful patrons. On weathered-wood decks overlooking the summer Atlantic. In a little inn among the hills and cliffs of Big Sur, California. Near noon on a hot weekday sitting at Sam's across the bay from San Francisco, looking back at the incomparable city, eating Eggs Benedict and drinking Bloody Marys while the boards groaned with the action of the water beneath us and people docking their sailboats at the landing stage, and seagulls threatening to take over. Once in the autumn high in the French Alps near Chartreuse at an extraordinary little inn called The Flowering-Hearth ("Auberge De L'Âtre Fleuri") run by two women of genius. As many times as I can arrange it, at the Pensione Accademia in Venice, a small ex-palace set at the confluence of two secondary canals with its front garden like a ship's prow pointing toward the Grand Canal several yards away. Breakfast of fruit and bread, coffee and tea, butter, jams and marmalade eaten in the warming sun at a table covered with a fresh pink or green cloth. (The Accademia was used as the setting for Katherine Hepburn's film *Summertime*.) One late summer and early autumn in a hillside house overlooking the ancient Spanish town of Tarragona on the Costa Brava. A delightful morning ritual of the milkman bringing the day's supply of milk followed by the breadman on his bicycle bringing our day's supply of bread. In a tiny, wonderful room with its own terrace on the top of the Hotel Welcome in Ville-Franche sur Mer, the scene in the thirties of expatriot writers, Jean Cocteau and American sailors on leave, the bay very still, the millionaires still asleep in their villas on Cap Ferrat, two small naval cruisers at anchor along with a sleek, black sailing yacht said to have belonged to Errol Flynn. At a luxury hotel just outside Zurich, set in its own golf course, with linen towels to greet our feet as they found the floor and bowls of red raspberries in cream to augment the marvelous coffee and *croissants* while we mused awake to the sunshine and the views across dark pines. Another breakfast—completely different—in a rustic summer lodge on a private lake in the land-o-lakes area of northern Wisconsin, but as luxurious with its fresh strawberries, hot pancakes, aromatic coffee. And boyhood mornings, early, before the July heat had mounted, with an apple, setting off across the fields to visit the neighbor's cows.

My sister Elizabeth Tilden remembers particularly breakfasts with her husband Bay and other members of her family aboard their boat *Sudan* in the tiny harbor of Fayette, Little Bay du Noc, in northwestern waters of Lake Michigan. This was in 1949 and they were cruising out of Ephrain, Wisconsin, north of Washington Island in Green Bay: "absolute peace and quiet . . . fresh cantaloupe, eggs and bacon and coffee—cooked on a bottle-gas stove in the galley . . . the only noise made by seagulls and fish popping out of the water." (Not so memorable; the hard roll and coffee—chocolate and fruit juice both cost extra—in convent school in Lake Forest, Illinois.) She remembers mornings in a room on the ninth floor of a hotel overlooking La Jolla, California, and the wide Pacific Ocean: "Double room with a dining table and chairs, kitchenette. Coffee provided (instant) with an electric wall-unit which operated when the two-cup pot was filled with water. Refrigerator and stove unit. . . . Everything available at nearby coffee shop/restaurant—wheatcakes and sausages, ham and eggs, potato cakes. . . . Loved the San Diego papers. Loved having the time to eat breakfast together. . . . Sunday brunch on the top floor of the hotel was great fun—champagne et al!" Another of her sea-going experiences was on a seventy-five-foot sports fishing boat chartered by friends Betty and Nick Saegmuller—"Breakfast was something *easy*. Loved frozen (Sarah Lee)-type cinnamon and caramel rolls with coffee, fruit or tomato juice. . . . Often had a half grapefruit practically plucked off the Florida trees. . . . We traveled down the inland waterway on stormy rough days just because it was more relaxing. The boat could go anywhere, but things had to be rigged for the sea (TV tucked into a corner with pillows bracing it, dishes in their special places, that sort of thing). We cruised past the keys and one of my favorites was the Boot Key Marina, Marathon. . . . Breakfast was always eaten in port, tied up at a dock. No one got up at a particular hour. We usually breakfasted in our robes in the dining salon and read the papers. The yacht had a captain and a first mate . . . because our hosts wanted to be free of that responsibility . . . there was piped-in stereo in the dining salon and the staterooms, kitchen area and bridge. None on the flying bridge, ha!''

Barbara Hall, a writer living in London, remembers a very disconcerting breakfast she experienced back in 1966 when she was invited as an official visitor by the government of Taiwan: ''I went from Zambia, the idea being that I'd write—as I did—for the *Guardian* and *Observer*, and also (which I didn't as they were temporarily estranged and Madame was in America) write a biography of Chiang's wife. I was taken to Quemoy for a day trip to see how the war against the mainland was progressing. It was a fairly cold one at that time, with bombardments of shells exchanged every other day—the shells containing propaganda leaflets. They also shouted to each other and played music to each other on loud speakers, etc. . . . On the flight over, our plane was buzzed, so it was decided not to fly back that night in case there were further incidents. So we had an unexpected overnight stop. I was the only visitor, and spent the night in the army officers' mess, a fine old building with a leaky roof. During the night a bombardment started and I thought it was just my luck to be on Quemoy when the long-awaited attack from the mainland began. But it was merely an electric storm of greater magnitude than usual. I'd had the forethought to put my dress and underclothes on a chair (the only piece of furniture apart from the bed), since water was streaming down the walls onto the floor.

''But I had also pushed the back of the chair against a wall so that at breakfast time I found all my clothes lying in a puddle. It was hot humid May weather and all I had with me was my white dress and underclothes. The dress had shrunk a bit, being of a synthetic material, but outwardly you couldn't tell it was dripping wet. Having no alternative I put it on. It was like being embraced by a frog that had leapt straight from the lily-pond and had not turned into a prince.

''I went into breakfast, where, luckily, we sat on cushionless wooden chairs. There were half a dozen officers and my interpreter. All men. For breakfast we had glasses of green tea, with the usual spinach-like trailing herbiage. We had soft fried eggs in batter, to be eaten with chopsticks. (Easier to eat if the chopsticks had been hollow like straws and you could have sucked the liquid egg up through them.) Finally, there were several long crisp sticks of what looked like barley sugar. These, my interpreter told me, were pigs' giblets.

"As a chaser, the officers each had a small glass of clear liquid which they said was a spirit made on the island, from sorghum. They dropped a lighted match in one glass and I watched the flame burn steadily until all the liquid had evaporated. I asked if I might have one too. (My need was greater than theirs.) I knew that when I got up from the wooden chairs I should be invited to sit on a sofa that was upholstered in pink satin. Next to it was a very low table holding the Visitors' Book, which I should have to sign. The general commanding the island had joined us and was waving me towards that sofa. If I sat on it, I should leave a wet patch. If I told him I couldn't sit on it because their roof had leaked in the night, they would lose face and I should be embarrassed. If I refused to sit, and tried to sign the book bent double from a standing position, they would think I was an eccentric Englishwoman.

"I stood, while we all made conversation for a long half hour, and I pretended not to understand each time solicitious gestures were made toward the sofa. Then we went on a tour of the island in an open jeep and I dried off."

Amid a Swiss landscape of glinting dark lake, sky of pewter and ivory—"presenting the sun's light without defining the star itself"—Ellen Ferber (in the January 1968 issue of *Gourmet*) watches an old man sweeping the street; the coffee's fragrance

A memorable morning? For the rooster perhaps, but not so for the poor dog beneath him. An illustration from Grandville's The Public and Private Life of Animals.

Boy with baguettes—a typical Paris morning scene, and always a memorable one.

merging with the chill pure air; the frothy hot milk; the flaky golden *croissants*; the apricot jam; rolls with "hard glazed surfaces and soft warm hearts"; strawberry jam the "exact shade of the tall peak called Pilatus as the sun stained its snow." It is one of what she calls the "true breakfasts of felicity."

Another is her first camping experience as a child: trout cleaned and deftly boned, coffee brewing ("don't forget the eggshell to settle the grounds"), bacon in an iron skillet. Biscuits browning in the coals beneath the fire. The bacon removed onto a brown paper bag to drain while the trout was dropped in with a sizzle. "The secret of cooking with bacon fat is immediacy, for if it cools and hardens it will have a stale and greasy flavor, ruinous to fresh lake trout." She prefers her trout between pieces of biscuit with a slice of bacon added. "The water laps against the beached canoes. There is a smell of Adirondack pine and smoke."

The thought of smoke reminds her of Dublin years later. Rain in October. Miserable. Wet and chilled in her hotel with a stingy electric fire that's all but useless. She drops disconsolately into an early bed. And then. . . . Breakfast on a tray. She glances dispiritedly under the dish covers—"Freshly squeezed, ice-cold orange juice in water tumblers. Irish soda bread, toasted and yellow with rich butter. Eggs and ham and country sausages grilled together and served in their earthenware cooking dish . . . ," the combination like "a kind of fresh smokiness, like the smell of clean dry leaves burning. . . The tea . . . is smoky too, almost black and almost bitter, but with no belligerence in the taste." The next morning the maid appears saying "I hope you fancy a wee kidney."

Ms. Ferber—like many of us—has her memories of Les Halles in early spring—onion soup, snails, pig's trotters; of "thick mocha chocolate and tiny crusty pastries" at the French Market in New Orleans among all-night revelers and tired night workers about to go home; "coral lox and mother-of-pearl whitefish and bagels and cream cheese" in a delicatessen off Broadway in New York. She recalls breakfasting on "lobster bisque at Boone's on the pier at Portland—the fisherman about to tackle his stack of wheatcakes topped by three fried eggs" and showing his disdain of anything as outlandish as lobster bisque for breakfast and saying nothing being a Maine man. Blueberry pancakes on Cape Ann with maple syrup from the northern forests. Eating "hot fried Ipswich clams from a paper bag . . . small, thinly coated with a light batter and cooked in butter," tasting of the sea, while watching the sun come up.

Ms. Ferber also shares my love for Venice—even alone: a solitary breakfast she's never forgotten—"A gilded morning in San Marco Square . . . pigeons endlessly repeating their daffy flight at each new ringing of the great tower bells . . . on the table only the clear topaz tea, a slice of lemon as large as the lushest Florida orange and pale as straw. . . ." She ends her recollections with a description of an unplanned breakfast, at the New Jersey shore, of leftovers from a beach picnic the night before: "sweet corn cut from its ears, juicy and uncharred from its previous roasting because it was wrapped in newspapers, shucks still on . . . dipped into the sea before cooking," the kernels dotted with butter and black pepper and grilled with "sliced roasted potatoes, thick circles of beefsteak tomatoes, and poppy seed rolls cut into thin rounds," a bowl of red raspberries in the center of the table. "At the last minute the bias slices of leftover cooked steak, brown at the edges and red in the center, are dipped momentarily into the skillet where browned butter and the remains of the Burgundy are simmering." And then there was her honeymoon breakfast with a snowstorm outside: "Canadian bacon, grapefruit laced with Cointreau, popovers, an applewood fire, and the *Sunday Times*."

A Breakfast Sampler

Thackeray wrote a book called THE YELLOW-PLUSH CORRESPONDENCE *in which he gave an account of society life in the vernacular of a cockney footman. He had such fun doing it that he often wrote letters in the same style :* "It is ate o'clock, we have had our brecfastes, are preparing our luncheses. I've had tea, brednbutter, coal-bile-biff."

Anthony Trollope in THE WARDEN (1855):

And let now us observe the well-furnished breakfast-parlour at Plumstead Episcopi, and the comfortable air of all the belongings of the rectory. Comfortable they certainly were, but neither gorgeous nor even grand; indeed, considering the money that had been spent there, the eye and taste might have been better served; there was an air of heaviness about the rooms which might have been avoided without any sacrifice of propriety; colours might have been better chosen and lights more perfectly diffused; but perhaps in doing so the thorough clerical aspect of the whole might have been somewhat marred; at any rate, it was not without ample consideration that those thick, dark, costly carpets were put down; those embossed, but sombre papers hung up; those heavy curtains draped so as to half exclude the light of the sun; nor were those old-fashioned chairs, bought at a price far exceeding that now given for more modern goods, without a purpose. The breakfast-service on the table was equally costly and equally plain; the apparent object had been to spend money without obtaining brilliancy or splendour. The urn was of thick and solid silver, as were also the tea-pot, coffee-pot, cream-ewer, and sugar bowl; the cups were old, dim dragon china, worth about a pound a piece, but very despicable in the eyes of the uninitiated. The silver forks were so heavy as to be disagreeable to the hand, and the bread-basket was of a weight really formidable to any but robust persons. The tea consumed was the very best, the coffee the very blackest, the cream the very thickest; there was dry toast and buttered toast, muffins and crumpets; hot bread and cold bread, white bread and oaten bread; and if there be other breads than these, they were there; there were eggs in napkins, and crispy bits of bacon under silver covers; and there were little fishes in a little box, and devilled kidneys frizzling on a hot-water dish; which, by the bye, were placed closely contiguous to the plate of the worthy archdeacon himself. Over and above this, on a snow-white napkin, spread upon the sideboard, was a huge ham and a huge sirloin; the latter having laden the dinner table on the previous evening. Such was the ordinary fare at Plumstead Episcopi.

A Music-hall song entitled "Oh, Why Is the Bacon so Tough?"

Oh, why is the Bacon so tough, tough, tough,
Oh, why is the Bacon so tough?
I'm taking this piece of rhinoceros-hide
To be built into a battle-ship down on the Clyde;
Every soldier and sailor could sleep safe in his
    bunk—
For a ship made of Bacon could *never* be sunk!
Oh, why is the Bacon so tough,
That's a question we're asking today . . .
Oh, why is the Bacon so tough?
It settles the argument, nay—
If Bacon wrote Shakespeare. . . .
TOUGH LUCK on the play!!!
Oh, why is the Bacon so tough?

From Evelyn Waugh's autobiography A Little Learning:
. . . There was a club in Balliol named the Hysteron-Proteron whose members put themselves to great discomfort by living a day in reverse, getting up in evening dress, drinking whisky, smoking cigars and playing cards, then at ten o'clock [one assumes A.M.] dining backwards starting with savouries and ending with soup.

. . . Once he had a dream in which one of us was convicted of the unknown vice of "vanoxism." It is John Sutro's recollection, but not mine, that it was connected with scourging raw beef with lilies. We founded a club named the Vanoxists who met for breakfast now and then at the Trout at Godstow, all of us united in nothing but affection for [the founder].

E. M. Forster in an essay titled "Porridge or Prunes, Sir?":
That cry still rings in my memory. It is an epitome—not, indeed, of English food, but of the forces which drag it into the dirt. It voices the true spirit of gastronomic joylessness. Porridge fills the Englishman up, prunes clear him out, so their functions are opposed. But their spirit is the same: they eschew pleasure and consider delicacy immoral.

In The Edwardians *J. B. Priestley writes:*
The Edwardian breakfast alone would make one of our Christmas dinners look meagre. First-comers arrived about eight o'clock, late-comers finished

eating about 10:30. There was porridge and cream. There were pots of coffee and of China and Indian tea, and various cold drinks. One large sideboard would offer a row of silver dishes, kept hot by spirit lamps, and here there would be poached or scrambled eggs, bacon, ham, sausages, devilled kidneys, haddock and other fish. On an even larger sideboard there would be a choice of cold meats—pressed beef, ham, tongue, gelatines—and cold roast pheasant, grouse, partridge, ptarmigan. (Harold Nicolson wrote: "No Edwardian meal was complete without ptarmigan. Hot or cold.") A side table would be heaped with fruit—melons, peaches and nectarines, raspberries. And if anybody was hungry, there was always scones and toast and marmalade and honey and specially imported jams.

The novelist Jean Rhys wrote in the London TIMES, *May 21, 1975,* "WHATEVER BECAME OF OLD MRS. PEARCE?":
For instance, I . . . wake very early; at the time of year I'm writing this it is still dark. I used to keep a book handy, put the light on and read, but now I've decided to save my eyes I get up instead, and, without looking at myself, stumble along the passage, switching lights on as I go. Then I am filling the kettle, taking the blue cap off its hook (careful, now, don't drop it), getting a saucer, spoon, sugar. From then on its routine.

After tea and cigarettes it gets lighter and I am happier. Perhaps the real deep feeling is of joy, even triumph, that one has survived the night.

Lewis Carroll as himself, the Rev. C. L. Dodgson, wrote home from a Continental tour in 1867:
We moved on to Giessen, and put up at the Rappe Hotel for the night, and ordered an early breakfast of an obliging waiter who talked English. "Coffee!" he exclaimed delightedly, catching at the word as if it were a really original idea, "Ah! coffee—very nice—and eggs? Ham with eggs? Very nice—" "If we can have it broiled," I said. "Boiled?" the waiter repeated, with an incredulous smile. "No, not boiled," I explained—"BROILED." The waiter put this distinction aside as trivial. "Yes, ham," I said, "but how cooked?" "Yes, yes, how cooked," the waiter replied, with the careless air of one who assents to a proposition more from good nature than from a real conviction of its truth.

In a collection of NORFOLK REMINISCENCES *(1971),
written by members of the Norfolk Federation of
Women's Institutes,* "WITHIN LIVING MEMORY":
Hard Times. Half an egg for breakfast—Drayton,
1912: My cousin used often to come to stay. We used
to share everything. He and I used to have half an
egg for breakfast or half a kipper cut lengthwise and
we never forgot whose turn it was to have the fat
side. How we enjoyed the homemade bread my
Granny made! We didn't have as much to choose
from as the children of today. They have so much
offered them they don't know what they want, I
sometimes think.

Some titles of popular songs naming breakfast—*none,
interestingly enough, famous:*
Breakfast at Home; Breakfast at Seven; Breakfast
Ball; Breakfast Club Adjourns; Breakfast Dance;
Breakfast Feud; Breakfast for Two; Breakfast in
Bed on Sunday Mornin'; Breakfast with You; Come
after Breakfast; Cooking Breakfast for the One I
Love.
And related titles:
Doughnuts and Coffee; Doughnut Song; Egg and I;
The Egg; Fried Eggs; Ham 'n' Eggs; Ham and
Eggs; Hot Biscuits; How Do You Like Your Eggs in
the Morning?; Let's Have Breakfast in Bed; Let's
Have Breakfast in Hollywood.

On their rock album "Atom Heart Mother," the
group known as Pink Floyd include a track called
"Alan's Psychedelic Breakfast" which contains a
startling passage of bacon being cooked—in
quadraphonic sound! And there's another track
called "Sunny Side Up."

RAMPARTS *reporting in August 1972 on things-
already-come:*
Among its lesser known contributions to American
life is ITT's invention of a breakfast cake for
children called Astrofood. Robert Cotten, vice
president for research at ITT's subsidiary Continental Baking, shrewdly and successfully per-
suaded the Agricultural Department to change the
guidelines governing the school breakfast program
so that ITT's new "engineered food" product,
Astrofood, would qualify. The idea is to replace
orange juice, milk, eggs and bacon with a cheap,
easily managed little cake, like a Twinkie. But
Astrofood is packed with synthetic vitamins and
proteins. In fact, according to enthusiastic food
engineers who are pushing this cake, all a kid needs is
one Astrofood and a glass of milk and he is better

141

behaved, more alert, and studies much harder.

As a result of the Agriculture Department's new rules permitting "engineered foods" in government-subsidized school programs, snack makers are racing into the market. ITT sells half a million Astrofood cakes every month to schools in St. Louis, Memphis, Little Rock and Atlanta. Tasty Baking Co., a recent market entry, sells 50,000 cakes a week to Philadelphia school children.

Some schools have rejected the engineered cakes. Nutritionists say "they cause cavities and teach youngsters to eat cakes instead of real foods." Others question the safety of large doses of synthetic vitamins contained in the yummy cream fillings. Because of their doubts New York schools rejected the new cakes.

In Waverley *(1841) Sir Walter Scott writes a good deal about breakfast :*
Waverley found Miss Bradwardine presiding over the tea and coffee, the table loaded with warm bread, both of flour, oatmeal, and barley-meal, in the shape of loaves, cakes, biscuits, and other varieties, together with eggs, reindeer ham, mutton and beef ditto, smoked salmon, marmalade, and all other delicacies which induced even Johnson himself to extol the luxury of a Scotch breakfast above that of all other countries. A mess of oatmeal porridge, flanked by a silver jug, which held an equal mixture of cream and buttermilk, was placed for the Baron's share of this repast.

Later Scott describes an "alfresco" breakfast :
. . . he found the damsel of the caravan . . . busy, to the best of her power, in arranging to advantage a morning repast of milk, eggs, barley bread, fresh butter, and honeycomb. . . . To this she now added a few bunches of cranberries, gathered in an adjacent morass. . . . Evan and his attendant now returned slowly along the beach, the latter bearing a large salmon-trout, the produce of the morning's sport. . . . A spark from the lock of his pistol produced a light, and a few withered fir branches were quickly in flame, and as speedily reduced to hot embers, on which the trout was broiled in large slices. To crown the repast, Evan produced from the pocket of his short jerkin a large scallop-shell, and from under the folds of his plaid a ram's horn full of whisky. Of this he took a copious dram.

Scott also throws a curious light on the breakfasting habits of the French in the days of the Auld Alliance when Scots served in France. Quentin Durward after his long fast was given this breakfast :
There was a *Paté de Perigord*, over which a gastronome would have wished to live and die, like

Homer's lotus-eaters, forgetful of kin, native country, and all social obligations whatever. . . . There was a delicate ragout, with just that *petit point de l'ail* which Gascons love and Scottishmen do not hate. There was, besides, a delicate ham, which had once supported a noble wild boar in the neighbouring wood of Montrichard. There was the most exquisite white bread, made into little round loaves called *boules* (whence the bakers took their French name of *boulangers*) of which the crust was so inviting that, even with water alone, it would have been a delicacy. But the water was not alone, for there was a flask of leather called *boittrine*, which contained almost a quart of exquisite *vin de Beaune* . . . .

"The best meal I have eaten," said the youth, "since I left Glen-houlakin. . . ."

"The Scottish Archers of the Guard eat as good a one, or better, every day," his host assured him.

Scott's predilection for writing particularly about breakfast might be explained by this passage from Lockhart's LIFE:

Breakfast was his chief meal. Before that came, he had gone through the severest part of his day's work. . . . His plate was always provided, in addition to the usual plentiful delicacies of a Scotch breakfast, with some solid article, on which he did most lusty execution—a round of beef—a pasty, such as made Gil Blas' eyes water—or, most welcome of all, a cold sheep's head, the charms of which primitive dainty he has so gallantly defended against the disparaging sneers of Dr. Johnson and his bear-leader. A huge brown loaf flanked his elbow, and it was placed upon a broad wooden trencher that he might cut and come again with the bolder knife. . . . He never ate anything before dinner, and at dinner he ate sparingly.

In John Betjeman's poem BUSINESS GIRLS *he shows them* "having baths in Camden Town" *with the morning trains* "shaking the area," *autumn's nip in the air, and* "precarious bathrooms/Jutting out from upper floors." *The women soak and watch the* "Flying clouds and railway smoke." *The last stanza goes:*

Rest you there, poor unbelov'd ones,
    Lap your loneliness in heat.
All too soon the tiny breakfast,
    Trolley-bus and windy street!

In another of his poems, IN MEMORY OF BASIL, MARQUESS OF DUFFERIN AND AVA, *Betjeman writes movingly,*

On such a morning as this
    with *The Times* for June the eleventh
Left with coffee and toast

"OH, MUM, THIS *IS* A DELICIOUS EGG. IT MUST BE PRE-WAR."

you opened the break-fast room window
And, sprawled on the southward terrace,
    said: "That means war in September."
The next stanza begins,
    Friend of my youth, you are dead!

*Haji Muhammad reported to the Venetian geographer,
Ramusio, in 1550 that tea was* "commonly used and
much esteemed" by the people of Cathay who "take
of this herb whether dry or fresh, and boil it well in
water. One or two cups of this *decoction* taken on an
empty stomach removes fever, headache, stomach
ache, pain in the side or in the joints, and it should be
taken as hot as you can bare it. . . ."

A French anecdote regarding BRIOCHE:
The expression *"faire une brioche"* means "to
blunder" because the members of the Paris Opera
orchestra, when they were flat or out of tune or
rhythm, had to pay a fine into a kitty which was used
to buy *brioches* for the entire orchestra during
rehearsals.

Anthony Trollope in DOCTOR THORNE *(1858):*
In these days a man is nobody unless his biography is
kept so far posted up that it may be ready for the
national breakfast table on the morning of his
demise.

Mark Twain in INNOCENTS ABROAD *(1869):*
I do not want Michael Angelo for breakfast—for
luncheon—for dinner—for tea—for supper—for
between meals.

From Susan Ferrier's MARRIAGE *(1818):*
"The breakfast!" exclaims Dr. Redgill . . . "that's
what redeems the land—and every country has its
peculiar excellence. In Argyllshire you have the
Lochfyne herring, fat, luscious, and delicious, just
out of the water, falling to pieces with its own
richness—melting away like butter in your mouth.
In Aberdeenshire you have the Finnan haddo' with a
flavour all its own, vastly relishing—just salt enough
to be piquant, without parching you up with thirst.
In Perthshire there is the Tay salmon, kippered,

crisp and juicy—a very magnificent morsel—a *leetle* heavy, but that's easily counteracted by a teaspoonful of the Athole whisky. In other places you have the exquisite mutton of the country made into hams of the most delicious flavour; flour scones, soft and white; oatcakes, thin and crisp; marmalade and jams of every description.

Sir Walter Scott in a letter to his son-in-law, J. G. Lockhart, who was in London (December 20, 1825):
What meal does Johnie want for his porridge? [Johnie being Scott's grandson] I will send it up from Abbotsford. I think it will agree with him better than the southern food for horses.

The admirable Mrs. Beeton in her COOKERY BOOK :
We are all creatures of example, servants and children being no exception to the rule, and it is seldom that a late mistress does not make a late household.

There is no work like morning work, particularly household tasks, and those we take up early in the day, when fresh from a night's rest and a good breakfast, are "trifles light as air" in comparison with the same dragged or hurried through later when there is not time for their proper performance.

Dr. Maurice Fagan, director of General Foods Center for Applied Nutrition :
Nature doesn't have the quality control our plants have. We can measure Vitamin C into Tang quite precisely. But oranges vary in Vitamin C content.

Rudyard Kipling in "GEORGIE PORGIE" *(from* LIFE'S HANDICAP; BEING STORIES OF MY OWN PEOPLE, *1891):*
He did not rave, as do many bridegrooms, over the strangeness and delight of seeing his true love sitting down to breakfast with him every morning, "as though it were the most natural thing in the world." "He had been there before," as the Americans say.

Breakfast-time in the Monkey-House.

"Breakfast-time in the Monkey-House"—a Victorian children's jigsaw puzzle.

Breaking the Pattern

> "It frequently breakfasts at five-o'clock tea,
> And dines on the following day."
> *The Hunting of the Snark*
>
> Food that is good for you is good for you at
> any time.
> *The Good Breakfast Book*

Try for a change, change itself.

An American family, tired of never being able to be together for dinner, all got up early and had their dinner in the morning. Try eating things you've never associated with breakfast. Try eating breakfast in a different place. Pauline de Rothschild, one of the great hostesses of this century, never served a meal in the same place on the same day, but moved all over the house.

You can eat anything for breakfast. That is, anything your heart, or rather, your stomach desires. Actually, your heart *does* play an important role. If you love certain foods it is fairly obvious that your day will begin a happier one if you eat what you love. If I could afford it, I would start the day with a grilled steak or two or three lamb chops or *prosciutto* and melon or pears. I've been told of those who embrace chocolate cake and a Coke. There are partisans of pie—apple or otherwise (and why not? how is it different from the commonplace coffee cake

usually included?). One tires of food tyrants, watch-and-warders, cuisine commandos, digestion dictators with rules for everything, strict dos and don'ts. I've seen people relishing radishes, cold macaroni, lentil soup (delicious on a cold winter's morn), cucumbers and sour cream.

So make a change. Skip lunch and take that hour for breakfast and see how you feel. Here are some suggestions to get you going along with a few recipes for you to try your hand at.

Try soups—the Japanese eat them every morning—hot, substantial ones on cold mornings; cool, refreshing ones on a summer's day (many of them can be made in advance and stored). Minestrone or cream of chicken, vichyssoise or gazpacho (see "The Morning After"). Try a salmon soufflé, or one of chicken, or lemon (but not sweet), or orange, or mushroom instead of the expected omelette. Have fish *au gratin*, baked in the oven. A plate of ratatouille made with all the vegetables in season you adore. If you live alone, eat your omelette straight out of the pan.

Serve the kids fishcakes made the night before from poached and flaked coley, instant mashed potatoes, chopped parsley and anchovy essence rolled in flour and fried in bacon fat. Have bacon with them. (One of several ideas of Harold Wilshaw in the *Guardian*, October 3, 1975). A few others: serve sweetbreads with bacon or brains steeped, blanched and demembraned the night before, sliced and fried in butter. Poach cod in water and milk with a bay leaf—you can also poach an egg, after, in the same water. Lamb's liver is quick to fix. Try vegetable leftovers, reheated and mixed with eggs or just plain.

Make a cold grapefruit soufflé or one of grapefruit, shrimp and asparagus. Cook a cauliflower, drain it upside down in a bowl to retain its shape, then serve it cold with giant shrimps interspersed between the flowers. Make a terrific Italian spaghetti called *putanesca* (after prostitutes who stir up a batch between customers because it's cheap and fast). It's good left over too. *Playgirl* (February 1976) offers a "walk-away health breakfast" full of vitamins and quick to make: ½ cup orange juice, two eggs, one tablespoon of honey or to taste—blend.

Make yourself a real hamburger of the best chopped meat, a garden-ripe tomato, lettuce, mayonnaise and an onion or other garnish you like best. If you're in the area, indulge yourself in a fresh lobster or any of the just-caught fish in neighboring waters. I remember eating an incredible salmon that I saw being unloaded from a just-returned fishing boat in a waterside restaurant along the coast north of San Francisco. *Woman's Wear Daily*, that critical, lively and enthusiastic rag, printed a series of imaginative alternatives by Doris Tobias. Stuff thin Russian *blini* of buckwheat flour with thinly sliced double-smoked Nova Scotia salmon, a few sprigs of dill, served on heated plates with sour cream, and lemon and tea in glasses. Make a sauce of garlic (one clove), seeded chopped tomatoes (two or three), finely chopped parsley (handful), salt, pepper, cooked over low heat, poured over eggs (one dozen) in a butter-greased casserole with freshly grated Romano cheese added, and bake until eggs are set. Fill a bowl with cubes of pineapple and sliced Comice pears (with skins on). Slice raw tenderloin of beef very thin, sauté quickly in butter with some finely chopped shallots and mushroom duxelles just until beef loses its bright red; season with salt, pepper, dash of Worcestershire and fold into warm crêpes; warm a little Cognac, ignite and pour, flaming, over crêpes. Extravagantly: "set mini glasses of Sevruga caviar into bowl-shaped wine glasses half-filled with crushed ice. Accompany each with a pony of icy Pertsovka vodka. Set small trays of chopped white onions and bowls of thick sour cream in front of each place. Serve a huge loaf of thickly sliced black Russian pumpernickel and crocks of sweet country butter. Follow with strong hot tea and chunks of raisin babka."

Or you can take a tip from the Scandinavians and set out a number of separate dishes—all cold or all hot or half and half. Smoked fish, cold meats, salads, shrimp and watercress, cooked, diced beets mixed with potatoes in a cream and lemon dressing. Combine chicken or turkey broth (three cups), ¼ cup minced celery, one tablespoon minced onions, one tablespoon chopped parsley and bring to boil.

Sprinkle in (one cup) cream of rice, stir, cook for 30 seconds. Remove from heat, cover and let stand five minutes. Stir in one cup finely chopped chicken or turkey. Pour into lightly oiled loaf pan. Chill for about eight hours. Unmold and cut into slices. Dust with flour and brown in skillet with a little oil. Serve with cheese sauce or stewed tomatoes.

Serve a classic Spanish *paella* of lobster, prawns, clams or cockles, oysters, garlic-seasoned pork sausage, chicken, pork, onions, garlic, peppers, tomatoes, rice, saffron, peas. Drink a cool fruit-and-wine *sangria* with it. Try baked pumpkin with beef, a Latin American dish. Or an avocado cream soup. The idea is to take a chance.

F. Marian McNeill's Findon Haddock

Skin a Findon haddock and cut it in pieces. Lay these on a stewpan with a dessertspoonful of butter. Put the lid on tightly and steam for five minutes. Now break a teaspoonful of cornflour with a little milk, and add more milk—a breakfastcupful in all. Pour over the fish and butter, bring to the boil, and boil for a minute. Take out the pieces of fish, lay them nicely on a dish, and pour the sauce over them.

Smoked haddock may be served with a poached egg or a daub of whipped cream. Note: To skin a haddock, hold it before the fire for a short time; then lay it on the palm of one hand and clap it with the other. You will find that if you begin at the head the skin will come off easily without breaking the fish.

F. Marian McNeill's Scots Omelette . . .

Take some fresh herring milts; salt them, sprinkle with cayenne, and with finely chopped chives, parsley and chervil. Wrap each milt in a thin slice of smoked salmon, and poach in butter. Set them aslant in the center of an omelette *aux fines herbes*, and roll up. Serve immediately.

. . . and Scots Eggs

Boil the eggs hard as for salad. Peel them, dip them into beaten egg, and cover with pork sausage-meat. Egg-and-breadcrumb them, and fry for ten minutes in deep fat. Serve with or without a gravy sauce.

J. Walter Flynn's Cold Grapefruit/Shrimp/Asparagus Soufflé *(from* CARTE BLANCHE *magazine for Jan.-Feb. 1976)*

In top of double boiler, sprinkle two envelopes of unflavored gelatin over $\frac{1}{2}$ cup fresh grapefruit juice. In small bowl, mix together four egg yolks and remaining $\frac{1}{2}$ cup grapefruit juice; stir into gelatin. Place over boiling water and stir constantly until gelatin dissolves and mixture thickens slightly (about five minutes). Remove from heat. Purée asparagus (15-ounce can of spears drained) with $\frac{1}{2}$ onion in blender. Stir asparagus mixture, $1\frac{1}{4}$ teaspoons of salt, 1 teaspoon of sugar, $\frac{1}{4}$ teaspoon dried dill weed, $\frac{1}{8}$ teaspoon hot pepper sauce into grapefruit mixture. Chill, stirring occasionally, until mixture mounds slightly when dropped from a spoon. Add $\frac{3}{4}$ teaspoon of cream of tartar to egg whites in a small bowl and beat until stiff but not dry. Fold into gelatin mixture along with 1 pound cooked, clean shrimp, finely chopped (about $2\frac{1}{4}$ cups) and $1\frac{1}{2}$ cups of grapefruit sections. Turn into a one-quart soufflé dish with a two-inch collar. Chill several hours until set. Remove collar to serve. If desired, garnish with whole shrimp and dill or parsley sprigs.

Several of Nikki and David Goldbeck's Breakfast Variations

Cottage Cheese and Vegetables : Allot $\frac{1}{2}$–1 cup cottage cheese per person depending on appetites. Combine the cottage cheese in a bowl with lots of chopped green pepper, minced scallion, sliced radish, grated carrot, diced celery, adding or eliminating to suit your taste. Top with a heaping spoonful of yogurt. Some people add a few raisins for variety, and the smart ones add a thick topping of wheat germ. Warm cottage cheese and vegetables over gentle heat.

Broiled Tomato and Cheese : Slice four medium tomatoes into three thick slices each. Broil on one side. Turn. Combine two cups cottage cheese and one cup shredded cheese (Cheddar, Swiss, Gouda, or Provolone) to taste. Pile in mound on ungrilled side of tomato. Sprinkle with two tablespoons of wheat germ and broil until cheese bubbles. Allow two to three tomato slices per serving.

Mary Janes (the kids can help with this one) : With a shot glass or cookie cutter, cut a small hole in the center of a slice of whole-grain bread. Brown the bread lightly on one side in hot fat, turn the bread over, and break an egg into the center hole. Cook until yolk begins to set on the bottom, flip, and cook briefly to set. Don't forget to sauté the small round bread that has been removed—the "dunky"—along with the eggs. Use it to sop up the yolk.

"Gothic" Brunch : Drain liquid from two cups canned salmon (1 pound) and add enough skim milk to it to equal 1 cup. Sauté 2 tablespoons chopped onion in oil until tender and transparent. Remove from heat and, using a wire whisk, stir in 2 tablespoons of cornstarch to make a smooth paste. Add liquid and stir over moderate heat until thickened, 5 to 10 minutes. Season with pepper, stir in cottage cheese, and heat, stirring gently, until cheese melts. Add salmon, stir, warm, and serve immediately. Makes four servings.

Basic Whole-Wheat Griddlecakes : Mix $\frac{3}{4}$ cup whole-wheat flour, 2 tablespoons wheat germ, 2 teaspoons baking powder, $\frac{1}{2}$ teaspoon salt, 6 tablespoons nonfat dry-milk powder. Add 1 cup water, 1 tablespoon honey, 1 lightly beaten egg, and 1 tablespoon oil, and mix just enough to moisten all ingredients. Pour batter onto preheated, lightly oiled griddle or skillet, allowing about $\frac{1}{4}$ cup batter per pancake. When bubbles appear, turn and brown other side. Makes 10 3-inch pancakes.

Green Tahini Soup: Bring $5\frac{1}{2}$ cups of water to boil; add 2 teaspoons salt and $\frac{1}{2}$ cup couscous or pastina and cook five minutes, until grain is tender. Beat $\frac{1}{2}$ cup sesame-paste tahini with remaining $\frac{1}{2}$ cup water and pour into hot soup, stirring constantly. Add juice of $\frac{1}{2}$ lemon. If tahini is not available, substitute peanut butter. Makes four servings.

Eggless Griddlecakes: Same as above but add $\frac{1}{2}$ teaspoon baking powder and two tablespoons soy flour to the dry ingredients and eliminate egg.

Griddlecakes with Fruit or Nuts: Add $\frac{1}{4}$ cup chopped walnuts, raw cashews, peanuts, pumpkin seeds, or sunflower seeds, or $\frac{1}{4}$ cup sliced fresh banana, peaches, berries, or well-drained canned crushed pineapple to basic recipe.

Mrs. Beeton's Cornish Pasties

First prepare a short pastry: sift together 8 ounces plain flour, pinch of salt; rub 2 ounces butter and 2 ounces lard lightly into flour, using fingertips; then mix to a stiff paste with cold water. Set dough aside. Next mince $\frac{1}{4}$ pound raw meat finely. Dice $\frac{1}{4}$ pound potatoes. Add $\frac{1}{2}$ teaspoon finely chopped onion, mixed herbs to taste, salt, pepper and 2 tablespoons gravy or water. Mix well together.

Divide pastry into eight equal portions and roll out to $\frac{1}{4}$-inch thick, keeping portions as round as possible. Pile mixture in center of each pastry, wet edges and join together on the top to form upstanding frill, prick with a fork. Bake in hot oven (425° F) for 10 minutes, then reduce heat to moderate (350° F) and cook for about 50 minutes longer.

Elizabeth Van Loewen's "Putanesca" Spaghetti

Fry a clove or two of garlic in light oil. Pour in one 15-ounce can of peeled tomatoes. Add about $\frac{1}{2}$ pound of de-boned anchovies (preferably in salt rather than in oil), some oily black Greek olives (about $\frac{1}{4}$ pound) de-stoned and halved, a handful of dried, salted capers (if obtainable). Stew together for a while. Season with salt and lots of freshly ground black pepper. Serve with spaghetti which has been cooked in unsalted water.

For a Sunday breakfast of leftover *putanesca*, put some olive oil in a frying pan, add a beaten egg to the spaghetti and cook slowly until it forms a crust on bottom. Place a plate over the pan and turn the mixture over to cook on other side. Cut like a cake and serve.

The author's tribute to the first meal of the day.

Song of Morning Coffee

Hello. It is a good day.
A bowser walks a boy on a chain.
No chance of rain. Clear skies.

I am praying the morning paper
which has sounds of praise in it.
It welcomes the fact of the visitor-sun
always coming to call.

"Clear skies" it says here in the *Times*.
I see it's true. I agree.
Skies fit for Aristophanes' silly birds to meet in.
Skies for the likes of me.
I thank you.

I think when I finally wake up
I'll be a person more than I am,
be ideal, be better able to grasp the situation
(which is a sunny morning),

to say, not just words, but to speak,
to sit as a sitter, to drink as a drinker,
to be able to sing my little song:

My beard is on my razor
My coffee's in its cup
The ghost's well-hid in the draperies
I'm up

Best to keep at it. It would
be stupid to let it go.

The hot liquid travels.

The sun fondles.

Forget the honest voices of night!

Acknowledgments

I wish to thank various persons and organizations for their generous help in supplying information and visual material for this book—most especially, Donna Lubell, Maurice Broadbent, Elizabeth Tilden, Colin Thurlow, Leo Somers, Barbara Wecott, Barbara Hall and Edward Field. I would also like to thank the editor Diane Flanel and the designer of the book Colin Lewis.

The publishers and myself also wish to acknowledge the following for permission to use material in this book.

Associated Book Publishers Ltd. and A. D. Peters & Co. Ltd for the excerpt from *A Little Learning* by Evelyn Waugh, published by Chapman and Hall Ltd.

Curtis Brown Ltd. for the excerpts from *A House and Its Head* (1936) by Ivy Compton-Burnett. Reissued by Gollancz in 1966.

J. M. Dent & Sons and Little, Brown and Company for "The Eight O'Clock Peril" by Ogden Nash. From *Verses from 1929 On* by Ogden Nash. Copyright 1936 by Ogden Nash.

Farrar, Straus & Giroux, Inc., and Secker & Warburg Ltd. for the excerpt from *Sido and My Mother's House* by Colette, translated by Enid McLeod and Una Vincenzo. Translation copyright 1953 by Secker and Warburg.

Fontana Paperbacks for excerpts from *Eat Fat Grow Slim* by Richard Mackarness (1975).

William Heinemann Ltd. and Harper and Row, Inc., for the excerpt from *The Edwardians* by J. B. Priestley.

Little, Brown and Company for the extract from *The Country Kitchen* by Della Lutes. Copyright 1936 by Della Lutes. Copyright © 1964 by Mary Jane Lutes Putnam.

Macdonald and Jane's Publishers Ltd. for the extract from *Food in England* by Dorothy Hartley, published in 1954.

Macmillan Publishing Company for "Song of Morning Coffee" by Ralph Pomeroy. From *In the Financial District* by Ralph Pomeroy. Copyright © 1968 by Ralph Pomeroy.

W. W. Norton & Company, Inc. and André Deutsch Ltd. for the excerpts from *Voyage in the Dark* by Jean Rhys (1968).

Oxford University Press for the excerpt from *Marriage* by Susan Ferrier, edited by Herbert Foltinek (1971).

The Times, London, for the extract from "Whatever Became of Old Mrs. Pearce?" by Jean Rhys in *The Times*, May 21, 1975.

The Viking Press for "Breakfast" by John Steinbeck. From *The Portable John Steinbeck*. Copyright © 1971 by The Viking Press.

Stella D. Webb (Stella Gibbons) for the extract from her *Cold Comfort Farm*, published by Penguin.

Recipe Index

About the Author

Ralph Pomeroy is a poet, painter, art critic, teacher and writer. He has been Travel and Entertainment Editor for *House and Garden*; has worked in a number of art galleries; been a university professor; exhibited as a painter; and lectured on art. As an art critic he has been on the editorial staff of *Art News* in America and *Art & Artists* in England, and has contributed to many other art publications.

His poems have been widely published in magazines both in the United States and Great Britain and he is represented in more than a dozen poetry anthologies, among them *The New Yorker Book of Poets* and *A Controversy of Poets*. Three books of his verse have been published: *Stills & Movies* (1961); *The Canaries as They Are* (1965); and *In The Financial District* (1968). His other published books include: *Soft Art* (1969); *Stamos* (1974); and *The Ice Cream Connection* (1975).

"Feed me with food convenient for me."

Book of Proverbs